Basic Computing
Principles

Third Edition

NCC Blackwell

First published 1994

First published in USA 1994

Editorial office: NCC Blackwell Ltd., Oxford House, Oxford Road, Manchester M1 7ED, UK

NCC Blackwell Ltd
108 Cowley Road
Oxford OX4 1JF
UK

NCC Blackwell Ltd
238 Main Street
Cambridge, Massachusetts 02142
USA

First published in 1987 as *Fundamentals of Computing*, edited by Graham Rowntree.
Second edition published in 1991.
This fully revised and updated edition published in 1994.

British Library Cataloguing in Publication Data

British Library data is available

American Library of Congress Data

Library of Congress Data is available

Typeset in 10pt on 11pt Palatino by ScribeTech Ltd
Printed by

ISBN 1-85554-209-9

This book is printed on acid-free paper.

Acknowledgements

Thanks go to NCC Blackwell for the publication of this book, to Stella Simpson and Karen Woods, the editorial staff, for their work in checking and proofreading material.

Thanks to Rex Wilton for his invaluable help in the preparation of this revised edition.

Thanks are also due to Ms Linda Knight for the illustrations.

Finally, thanks go to Mrs Margaret Wilson who typeset the second edition of this book.

Contents

Preface

This book is part of a series of six publications designed to form the basis for the International Diploma in Computer Studies Certificate awarded by NCC. However, the book can be used independently of the series and offers a helpful introduction to systems analysis for trainee analysts and computer programmers.

Little previous knowledge of computing is anticipated by the book, apart from a basic understanding that computers use programs to process data from input devices, and produce the output on some other mechanism and that information may be stored on magnetic tape or disk for subsequent use by the computer.

Computer hardware (the machinery) is developing rapidly and the associated software (the programs) is also subject to the same evolutionary process, although perhaps not at the same rate as the hardware. It would be impossible to detail every development and, indeed, that is not the purpose of the book.

The aim is to provide an understanding of both hardware and software and the facilities they provide, so that systems analysts and designers can exploit them when designing systems. Obviously a certain level of detail must be provided in order to demonstrate the strengths and weaknesses of each type of hardware, software, system or file option.

It is important that the analyst or designer understands the principles behind the features so that as the technology develops he or she may be able to appreciate the implications of those developments for systems design.

The first three chapters in the book look at the hardware in terms of the computer, methods of storing data and input and output devices. The book also considers data communication systems and the software available to support the operation of the machine and the development of application systems.

The book concludes with a look at the various system options available to the designer and discusses their advantages and disadvantages.

At the end of each chapter are exercises for the students to attempt. An appendix provides sample questions from past NCC Threshold/Diploma examination papers for the students to try with guidance from tutors.

1 Micros to mainframes

OBJECTIVES

When you have worked through this chapter, you should be able to:

— note how mainframes, minis, and micros differ, and the significance of networking and distributed processing

— list the main parts of a digital computer and their functions

— outline the action of a computer's central processor (CPU) during a machine cycle

— distinguish between, with examples, bits, bytes and words

— list the different possible meanings of a byte

— distinguish between RAM and ROM, and outline some major addressing systems.

INTRODUCTION

This chapter discusses the basic computer architecture and how data is represented within the computer.

The two major factors which stimulate development in any field are:

— the demands of users and potential users

— the technology available.

The interaction of these two factors can clearly be seen in the development of computers. Following the industrial revolution and the development of societies highly dependent on technology, the demands for more automated processes has increased rapidly. At the same time the dramatic developments in electrical, electronic and communications engineering, together with software expertise has enabled many of these demands to be met.

1.1 SOME BACKGROUND

We can describe the first three generations of computer hardware in terms of

1

the basic electronic units that provide the arithmetic and logic power. These units are, in turn, electron tubes (valves — large, fragile, power-hungry units) transistors (much smaller devices based on semiconductor physics), and integrated circuits ("chips"— tiny scraps of semiconductor with thousands, even millions, of transistors in the surface). The first generation (valve-based hardware) started to be replaced by the second generation (using transistors) in the late 1950s and early 1960s. Integrated circuits had appeared by then, so it was not long before third generation systems appeared.

The move from valves to chips brought:

— much reduced component size — the process of miniaturisation

— much increased reliability — with uninterrupted working times raised from a few minutes to tens of thousands of hours

— much reduced power demand

— much increased working speed

— hugely reduced purchase and running costs.

The micro (personal computer) appeared in the early 1970s. We can now buy such machines the size of a book, with hundreds of times the speed, computing power and memory capacity of the enormous machines of the 1950s and 1960s.

The fourth and fifth generations of computers are less clearly defined. It could be said that the fourth generation is based on technology, and the fifth on technology dependent application. Large Scale Integration (LSI) and Very Large Scale Integration (VLSI) technologies involve packing more processing power on a single chip, and the "transputer" takes this farther by packing many complete tiny processors together allowing them to operate simultaneously, giving access to parallel processing instead of the sequential processing offered by all earlier approaches. The size of the data unit handled has also grown (particularly in micro- and minicomputers), the eight-bit "byte", is no longer a restriction, since in 1979 the Intel 8086 processor used 16 bits, and now 32 bit processors are readily available. All this can be called the fourth generation.

The fifth generation is more conceptual than real, yet, but is normally taken to refer to fully developed artificial intelligence (AI) which can simulate normal human abilities of sight, hearing and touch, and which can learn and make deductions from past events. Some aspects already exist, in robotics and "expert systems" areas, but much more development can be expected.

Communications

Because of the large size of the early computers they were called mainframes. The term is still used for the large computers of today. However, in 1957 a company in the United States, Digital Equipment Corporation (DEC) was set up to produce smaller and more robust machines. These machines became known as minicomputers. The first really popular minicomputer was the PDP8, launched in 1965. Minis handle fewer users and tasks at a time than mainframes.

Most early mainframes had no links outside their specially controlled, air-conditioned machine rooms. Programs and information were transported to the computer room, in the form of punched card or paper tape. A computer operator organised the workload into batches to be processed by the computer. Output was usually in printed form which was distributed back to the users. This was (and still is) known as batch processing. The input and output functions were nearly always more time consuming than the processing, which left the machine idle for long periods.

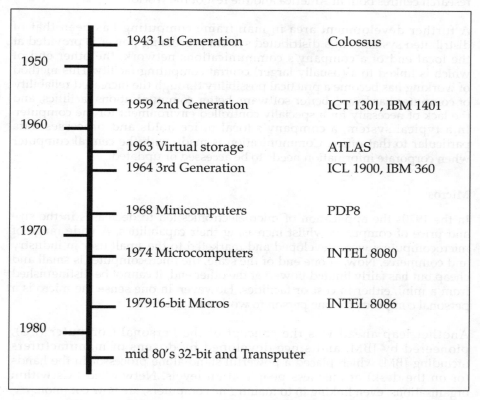

Figure 1.1   Major steps and machines in computing

The requirement to allow more than one program to share the processor so that the computer's resources could be utilised more efficiently was identified. Further, the need for users remote from the computer to have access to it was becoming more pressing. Project MAC at the Massachusetts Institute of Technology was set up between 1959 and 1962 to investigate these problems. The project, which was supported by several United States government agencies, developed the Compatible Time Sharing System, using IBM computers.

An example of developments using computer communications is an airline reservation system which provides a direct link between the booking clerk and a computer in a remote location. All the information being held is subject to constant change and must be accurate at the time an enquiry is made. This direct link is known as on-line communication. The process of ensuring that the information is updated immediately is called real-time. Real-time also describes the automated control of manufacturing processes, or indeed, any system where the computer must respond fast enough to influence the system of which it forms a part.

In the late 1960s, it became possible to link autonomous computers into networks through which information could be exchanged and resources shared. For example, ARPANET was developed to link universities and research centres both in America and the rest of the world.

A further development area in mainframe computing has been that of distributed systems. In a distributed system processing power is provided at the local end of a company's communications network, the other end of which is linked to a (usually larger) central computing facility. This method of working has become a practical possibility through the increased reliability of computer hardware, better software, better communications facilities, and the lack of necessity for a specially controlled environment for the computer. In a typical system, a company's local office holds and processes data particular to that office. Communication is made with the central computer when corporate information needs to be accessed or updated.

Micros

In the 1970s the application of microelectronics led to decreases in the size and price of computers whilst increasing their capabilities. A wide range of microcomputers were developed and marketed to the small user in industry and commerce. Now, at one end of the scale, the microcomputer is small and cheap but has fairly limited power; at the other end, it cannot be distinguished from a mini, either in cost or facilities. However, in one sense the micro is a personal computer, for one person to work with at a time.

Another leap ahead was the concept of the Personal Computer (PC), pioneered by IBM, and since developed by dozens of manufacturers including IBM, which placed a powerful stand-alone processor in the hands (or on the desk) of business people at all levels. Networked PCs within organisations, even linking in to mainframe computers, are now common.

Do not, however, assume that the microcomputer has superseded or become more sophisticated than the mainframe computer; both have their place in the development of business systems.

1.2 BASIC ARCHITECTURE

With computing systems and applications as diverse as they are today, the word *computing* itself covers a wide range of activities. Obviously a home computer for the hobbyist will differ greatly in power and facilities from the computer at the heart of an airline reservation system or the one monitoring and controlling a nuclear power station. However, the general principles are essentially the same, and the architecture remains that of the Analytical Engine designed by Babbage, with the addition of von Neumann's stored program concept.

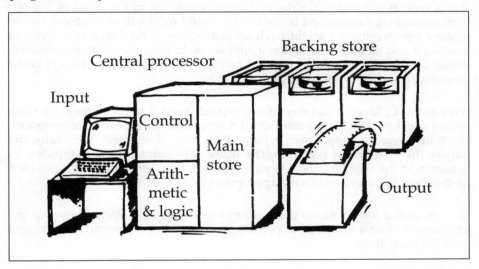

Figure 1.2 The parts of a computer

The basic parts of a computer are:

— an *input* unit which allows data to enter the machine

— a *main store* to hold the data and program instructions needed

— an *arithmetic and logic unit (ALU)* to perform the actual calculations (initially by cogs and wheels and now by microelectronics)

— a *control unit (CU)* which contains the sequence of tasks performed under direction from the stored program

— a *backing store* to hold data and programs not needed at the moment

— a means of *output* for sending the results of processing to the outside world.

In electronic computers the ALU and CU combine to form the central processing unit (CPU) or central processor.

Processing in the computer begins with the data and program or programs going into the store from the backing store and/or an input source; then the processes pre-set by the program(s) are carried out; and, lastly, the results are passed outside the computer system through some output device.

During this, each program instruction is fetched from store to the ALU, where it is interpreted. The ALU determines the addresses, (ie places) from which data is required, and the CU fetches the necessary data so that the ALU can complete the execution of the instruction. The CU then returns any data to store and fetches the next instruction. We call this a single machine cycle.

The speed at which a computer does these activities is based on its cycle time. For a typical minicomputer the cycle time would be in the order of 500-600 nanoseconds, a nanosecond being one thousand millionth of a second. In one cycle a microcomputer might fetch an instruction. It may take two cycles to decode it and then more to action it, and so on. In large mainframe computers these activities are done in parallel so that while one instruction is being decoded, a second is being fetched, and so on.

Within the CPU are a number of high-speed, special purpose memory units called registers which carry out critical functions in the execution of programs. Each architecture has its own type and number of registers. Generally, the larger the number of registers, the more sophisticated the computer. In addition to the registers, there is an instruction decoder which identifies each instruction and manipulates the appropriate ALU functions.

The processor also controls the bus or channel system which allows for the movement of data to and from peripheral devices (input, output and storage) and the main store.

The way data is transferred between the elements of the architecture has been developed into a full "bus" structure where the bus and its control are now a separate element of the architecture, with all other elements using the common bus for their own data transfer requirements. ("Bus" is taken from the public transport "omnibus"— a universal carrier with a predetermined route and opportunities for people to enter and leave when they wish. Note that an omnibus has a fixed maximum capacity — computer bus architecture can run up against capacity barriers too.)

The arrangement and control of the CPU varies from one computer to another. For example, some computers are controlled by a single processor whereas others may contain a number of processors, each controlling a different operation, eg input/output. The cycle time will vary, as will the degree to which the various activities within the CPU are overlapped. All these options give rise to the variety of computers which are available today. However, in all cases, the basic concept again follows that of the Analytical Engine.

1.3 DATA REPRESENTATION

The information or data processed by a computer is encoded in a particular way. The precise method of storing this information depends upon the type of computer. However, they all have some common characteristics.

The first common factor is the numbering system they use, which is different from that used by people. Where it is customary for numbers to be represented using ten different digits, computers are much less complex, using just two digits. The computer numbering system is called "binary" and the two digits with which its numbers are represented are "0" (nought) and "1" (one).

Binary

The binary numbering system is used because it can easily be represented in electronic circuitry, as it is equivalent to the "on" and "off" settings for lighting circuits.

The store of the CPU, even in a microprocessor, can hold thousands of these binary digits, or "bits" as they are called.

It is normal to arrange the bits into larger groups; each group can then be used to represent a number or character. The size of the grouping determines the number of code values available:

— 1 binary digit allows 2 codes (0,1)

— 2 binary digits allow 4 codes (00,01,10,11)

— 3 binary digits allow 8 codes (000,001,010,011,100,101, 110,111)

— 4 binary digits allow 16 codes (0000...1111)

— 5 binary digits allow 32 codes (00000...11111).

Bytes

The way that computers subdivide their total memory is their second common factor; most commonly used is a set of eight bits; or a "byte".

The number of different codes that can be made using the eight bits in a byte is 256. This number of codes is usually sufficient to represent all the different characters of which information may consist. Data can normally be represented by one byte per character. There is also, of course, a requirement to store instructions. Instructions may, however, need more than one byte to encode them. Thus whilst many instruction codes are represented using only one byte, others will require two, three or even four.

The position of data and instructions in the memory of the computer is not fixed and varies from program to program. In some cases the contents of a particular byte may be a character of data, in others it may be an instruction code or a part of such an instruction.

Words

Although subdividing data and computer memory into bytes is common, we also use the term "words"; in different machines the number of bits in a word varies. The word is the computer's basic unit of data, the unit concerned in data storage, processing and transfer. Thus, each bar must carry a word at a time.

Word lengths range from 8 bits to 64 bits, depending on the internal logic of the computer.

Data values

In a byte, each individual binary digit can be either "on" or "off" in electrical terms. These bit states are represented by the binary digits 1 and 0. A byte code may be represented by any combinations of bits from 00000000 to 11111111. Altogether there are 256 different patterns or codes that can be made with these 8 bits. The meaning of a byte code will depend upon whether or not that byte represents data or an instruction.

If the byte is a data code then it can still vary in its meaning according to what type of data it represents. It is most likely that the byte will represent one character of data, so a word like cat would be represented by 3 bytes, one for each letter. The most normal codes used in storing data within CPU memory as well as elsewhere are those based on the American Standard Code for Information Interchange (ASCII). Even numeric data may be stored in this way, ie one byte per digit. However, when calculations are to be carried out on stored numeric values, many machines convert the decimal value to its equivalent in binary. For large values more than one byte will be needed. Converting numeric data stored in character form to the equivalent in pure binary value and back again would be a normal part of a program. Holding numeric data in pure binary not only means that calculations will be carried out more quickly, it also means that less memory will be required to store the information.

Finally, there are some machines that allow numeric data to be held in a sort of half-way house between pure binary and one byte per digit. This method of storage (sometimes known as "packed decimal") uses the fact that only four bits are required to make ten different binary codes to represent the decimal digits, and so each byte contains the representations of two digits.

Memory addressing

In order for a computer to operate, both the program and data must be in the main memory. The computer must be able to locate the program instructions and data exactly. To do this each subdivision of memory has an address (usually starting from zero). The smallest addressable unit in most machines is the byte.

The maximum number of main memory locations that may be directly addressed will vary considerably from computer to computer. In the smallest, it may be less than 1000, in the largest it will be measured in tens or hundreds of millions. For various reasons the size of the memory is measured in Kbytes for the smaller computer and in megabytes or Mbytes for the larger machines. To be exact, K is a measure of 1024 but is often interpreted as 1000, as in Kg for kilograms (1000 grams). Mega means 1,000,000.

As each location in memory is available by direct addressing, a reference to one location may be made just as easily as to any other. The term frequently used for CPU store is Random Access Memory or RAM. Programs are able to both read from and write to this type of memory. We therefore call it read and write storage or memory, RAM for short. In most modern computers there is also ROM (Read Only Memory). This is accessed in exactly the same way as

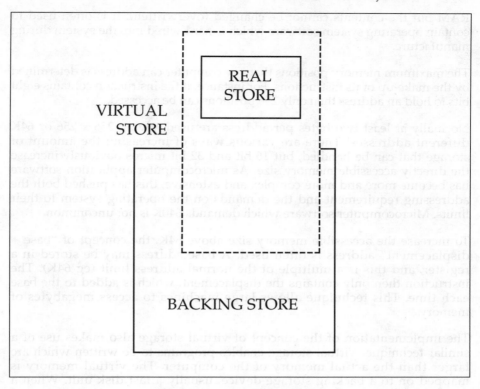

Figure 1.3 Virtual storage

Figure 1.4 compares various computers.

	Very large	Large	Medium	Mini	Large micro	Medium small micro
	CRAY Y-IMP	ICL 'ESSEX'	DG MV/ 2000-IT	DEC Micro vax 3400	(AT/386/ 486)	
CPU cycle time	6	10	16	20	37	410
Max. no. of Bytes (Mb)	1000	256	128	50	32	0.64
Word size (bits)	64	64	32	32	16/32	8/16
Cost	£15,000,000	£5,000,000	£1,000,000	£80,000	£1,500	£500

Figure 1.4 Comparison of CPUs

RAM but the contents cannot be changed (overwritten). It is often used to contain operating system software which is hard-wired into the system during manufacture.

The maximum memory positions that any computer can address is determined by the make-up of its instructions. For instance, if the instruction contains eight bits to hold an address then only 256 positions can be accessed.

Normally at least two bytes per address are used, giving 256 x 256 or 64K different addresses. There are various ways of increasing the amount of storage that can be handled, but 16 bit and 32 bit micros obviously increase the directly accessible memory size. As microcomputer application software has become more and more complex and extensive, this has pushed both the addressing requirement and the demands on the operating system to their limits. Microcomputer software which demands 640K is not uncommon.

To increase the accessible memory size above 64K, the concept of "base + displacement" address is often used. A base address may be stored in a register, and this is a multiple of the normal address limit (eg 64K). The instruction then only contains the displacement, which is added to the base each time. This technique allows large machines to access megabytes of memory.

The implementation of the concept of virtual storage also makes use of a similar technique. Virtual storage enables programs to be written which are larger than the actual memory of the computer. The virtual memory is mapped on to a backing storage device, usually a fast disk unit. When a particular segment of program (or data) is required, it is loaded into the real memory and the instruction address modified as required by varying the base register.

1.4 CONCLUSION

The development of computers has moved rapidly through three generations and is now in the fourth. The concept of a fifth generation is widely discussed. It will be based on knowledge based systems and Artificial Intelligence (AI).

The range of computers now available to the designer is wide. However, in choosing a particular system he should look not only at the present use of the data, but also possible future uses. The need for communications and the storing of data will play a major part in the future development of business systems.

The final choice must, however, be a system which meets the user's requirements.

NOW TRY THESE . . .

1   Explain the meaning of distributed processing. Explain briefly how distributed processing could bring advantages for either:

    (a) the computerisation of a national tax system, or

(b) the compilation of local editions of a large national daily newspaper.

2. Look inside a computer and identify the main printed circuit board and as many types of chip as you can. Find out the function of each type of chip and identify it as (for instance) processor, ROM, RAM, input/output control. If you can obtain a circuit diagram for the system, try to relate it to what you see and to Figure 1.2 (Block diagram of computer).

3. Explain how a computer differs from a cheap calculator. And from an expensive one.

4. Draw a block diagram of a computer, showing the directions of data flow; explain the function of, and need for, each part; sketch and name examples of each type of peripheral.

5. Give examples of five types of each hardware, software and firmware available for a micro used in your school, college or workplace.

6. Discuss the nature and uses of a mainframe, minicomputer, microcomputer and network.

2 Data storage devices

OBJECTIVES

When you have worked through this chapter, you should be able to:

— distinguish, with examples, between database, file and record

— explain why computers have both main and backing store

— outline the principal types of main and backing storage system

— describe magnetic tape systems and their use

— describe magnetic disk systems and their use, and compare them to tape

— briefly describe the nature and use of a remote batch terminal

— outline the methods involved in, and advantages of, key to store techniques

— describe the main features of VDUs

— outline the use of point of sale, factory, graphics, and cash receipt terminals, and of cash machines (autotellers)

— briefly describe and compare mark reading and optical and magnetic ink character reading

— outline the principles and problems of writing and speech recognition systems

— state what a sensor is, with examples, and with brief notes on use

— briefly describe the different types of character, line and page printer

— state the function of a plotter (graphics printer) and briefly describe the two main types

— outline the nature and use of computer output on microform.

INTRODUCTION

Data processing systems often require access to very large quantities of data. The computer's main (or immediate access) store is unsuitable for this task for two reasons. Firstly, the amount of data needed for any commercial system is too large to be held in the processor, and secondly, normal processor memory does not retain data if power is removed. Some form of backing storage is therefore required. This chapter looks first at the way data is grouped together and then at the storage media available. After that we turn to the rest of computer hardware (equipment), looking at the main data input and output units.

2.1 DATA FILES

Data or information is collected together into what, in most computer systems, is called a file. The other term frequently used for a set of data is a database, which could be defined loosely as a collection of interrelated files and their relationships. A file would normally be too large to process in one operation, and so the file is broken down into logical subdivisions called records.

To illustrate this, a file might contain information about the different items that a company manufactures. There would be a separate record for each item, each containing information such as an item number, a description, cost of manufacture, selling price, etc. Most computer files are like this, ie all the records in the file contain the same kind of information. Files may be set up containing different types of records, with different kinds of information, but even these will normally have some relationship with each other. For example, an invoice file might have three record types. First there could be a header record with customer information and invoice number, then from one to 20 (say) different records, each with the details of an item invoiced, including quantity and price, and then a summary record of a third type, containing Sales Tax calculations, delivery and packing information and the value totals. Then another header would be expected, more item records, another summary, and so on along the file.

2.2 STORAGE MEDIA

Data files are stored in (or on) whatever storage medium is available to that particular computer system, or, where there is a choice, that which produces the most efficient processing.

This chapter considers present and potential future methods of storage, firstly for main storage, then for backing storage.

Main storage is the internal storage provided within the CPU as described in the last chapter.

Backing storage is external to the CPU, connected to it by some kind of communication channel. It provides larger and cheaper storage facilities than the main store, and often uses a removable medium, allowing vast quantities of information to be kept, though only a limited amount can be accessed directly without some operator action to change the storage medium.

The cost of backing storage is directly related to the speed at which the data can be accessed. In order to process data from the backing store, it is necessary to transfer the data into the CPU and write it over ("overlay") part of the data or program previously held in the immediate access store.

Data can be stored on paper, magnetic media, film, optical disk, or semiconductor chips. To be useful to computer systems, the data must be readily written to or read from the storage medium. Printed paper is a good storage medium, as it is readable by both machines and humans. Unfortunately machine reading of printed material is still expensive and fairly slow. Paper is also bulky and difficult to organise. Microfiche or microfilm can be used in a similar way, and is much less bulky, easier to organise and to store; it is still, however, difficult and expensive to re-input information from microfilm to the computer. Hence the storage of data on microfilm is at present largely confined to long term storage (archiving). Such information is unlikely to change or be needed for regular retrieval and processing. Laser technology may in the future allow film storage with much improved access time.

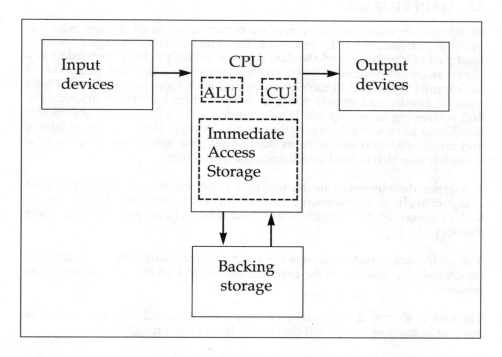

Figure 2.1 Computer storage

Laser technology has already led to the development of optical discs, which can be written by computer and much more cheaply read by computer. Again, at present, this is largely used for archival data, data which is unlikely to change. Updating of optical disk storage, since it is a medium which is difficult to alter once the data is recorded, tends to be done by producing a complete new version of the data. However, optical disk technology is developing, and the very high packing density allows vast quantities to be stored in a small space with easy access, so this may provide a major element of baking storage in the future.

At present, practically all backing storage devices other than chips use mechanical movement to locate data, and apart from the optical disk, use some form of electromagnetic recording. Electromagnetically recorded data can be erased and new data recorded in its place, so the medium is re-usable. The major differences between the devices are in the methods used to move the medium or the reading head (or both). The aim is to make the mechanism as simple and reliable as possible, while allowing the fastest achievable access to any specific item of data. The ultimate aim is to dispense altogether with any form of mechanism and to locate data entirely by electronic means. This has been achieved in main storage, but has not yet been achieved cheaply enough on a very large scale. However, the use of chips for backing storage, especially in laptop micros, is growing fast.

2.3   MAIN STORAGE

To operate at all, a computer needs a certain amount of storage which is directly addressable by the processor. This must be large enough to hold at least part of a program and the data which is actually being processed at any given instant. Access to such storage must be very fast (on today's mainframes measured in nanoseconds) and each location (ie group of bits) must be directly addressable. Costs of memory chips have fallen dramatically and addressing capability has been extended so that it is now economically feasible to have several megabytes of main storage. Hence many programs and much of their data can be in store at any one time. There may even be space left in which to hold small, frequently used files.

A further development is the use of a fairly small, extremely fast and comparatively more expensive "cache" memory connected directly to the CPU, backed up by a much larger, and relatively slower, cheaper main memory.

The addressing structure covers the main memory, with blocks of data and program being loaded by the machine hardware into the cache memory as required.

The cost of storing data has fallen dramatically. Figure 2.2 shows the cost of holding in main memory 2500 characters, from 1950 through to 1990.

The types of integrated circuit memory used are:

— RAM (Random Access Memory) which is used in the same way as previous main storage

— ROM (Read Only Memory) which has program instructions permanently "burnt in" at the manufacturing stage

— PROM (Programmable Read Only Memory) in which the user can "burn in" the bit patterns as required

— EPROM (Erasable Programmable Read Only Memory) which is similar to PROM but the "burning in" process is reversible, (erasing can take place by exposure to ultra-violet light).

It is interesting to note that the use of RAM and ROM allows the separation of program and data. There are advantages to this separation, for example the operating software does not need to protect the program from being overwritten by data.

To store 2,500 characters	Main memory £
1950	1,000,000
1960	30,000
1970	5,000
1975	1,000
1980	100
1983	30
1985	3
1990	0.50

Figure 2.2 Main storage costs

In microcomputers the use of ROM and RAM chips can be readily seen because of the simplified architecture, but in today's mainframe computers they are less obvious. ROMs are used, for example, to contribute to the "intelligence" of input/output controllers and terminal devices. they are often referred to as "firmware", being pre-programmed, and are simply replaced if there should be a need for change.

2.4 BACKING STORAGE

The most successful magnetic storage media in current use are the magnetic tape and the magnetic disk.

Magnetic tape

Magnetic tape has been used as a backing storage medium since the very early computers were produced. Today there are two basic type of magnetic tape devices in general use. The first is the standard computer tape which consists of ½" (12.7mm) wide plastic tape with a magnetic surface. Data is stored on it one character code at a time, each code using the full width of the tape (see Figure 2.3). The character codes are very close together, allowing 1600 or more characters for each inch (25.4mm) length of tape. A single 2400 foot reel of tape can hold millions of characters of data so the tape needs to be stopped and started as the data is required.

The second is the cassette or cartridge, rather like that used in modern audio tape recorders. Data is stored on this in a serial fashion, ie one bit following another; we'll come back to this type shortly.

As anyone who has a magnetic tape music player knows, starting the tape in the middle of a song produces an incorrect sound, because initially the tape passes the pickup head at the wrong speed, as it accelerates from rest. In the same way, data would "sound" wrong to the computer if it were read at the wrong speed. So, if the tape needs to be stopped and started, there must be no data in the length of tape passing the heads during deceleration and acceleration. This gap between units of data needs to be about ¾" (19mm) to allow the mechanism to operate without over stressing the tape.

Logically, it might seem that a stop/start gap should follow every data record in the file, but a data record might have 80 characters which only occupies $^{1}/_{20}$" (1.2mm) of tape. There would be 15 times as much "gap" as data, which is absurd. To overcome this, data records are collected together in some convenient unit and transferred in one pass. This is the "data block". The larger the block, the less waste of space on the tape, but the larger the memory requirement. A compromise block size is about 2000 characters.

Once the data is in the CPU, the program (or the operating system) enables each data record to be processed in turn, as though it had been read individually.

Although the use of magnetic tape has decreased as direct access storage devices (eg disks) have been developed, they still have a significant part to play in today's data processing systems.

Tapes are still ideally suited to serial processing of large volumes of data in mainframe systems. They are also inherently more secure than in fixed disks, as the only time they can be accessed is when they are loaded onto the computer. This is normally done by an operator who can check that the program requesting the file is authorised to do so.

Tape formats are more standard than disk formats. This makes them a good medium for the transfer of information between machines. Being smaller in size and physically less susceptible to damage than the disks used on mainframes, they can readily be transported between sites.

Backing up data on tape is also a cheap and effective way of providing security copies of files which can be stored off site. The arrival of the video tape — and other large capacity cassettes and cartridges — has given a new lease of life to cassette tape as a "back-up" medium, when a large non-removable disk is used in a computer, there is a need to copy some or all of the disk onto a secure medium at regular intervals in case of data corruption or malfunction. Tape streamers (as they are called) allow this to be done fast and efficiently.

2.5 MAGNETIC DISKS

Just as there is a wide variety of tape storage devices, there is also a wide range of magnetic disks and magnetic disk drives. In describing the characteristics of disks the terms *track, sector* and *cylinder* are used.

Tracks, sectors and cylinders

Regardless of the type of disk, all use the same method of storing data. The surface of the disk is divided into concentric circles known as "tracks" (see Figure 2.4). The number of these tracks will vary according to the diameter of the disk and the quality of the disk drive, and can range from about 40 to over 2000.

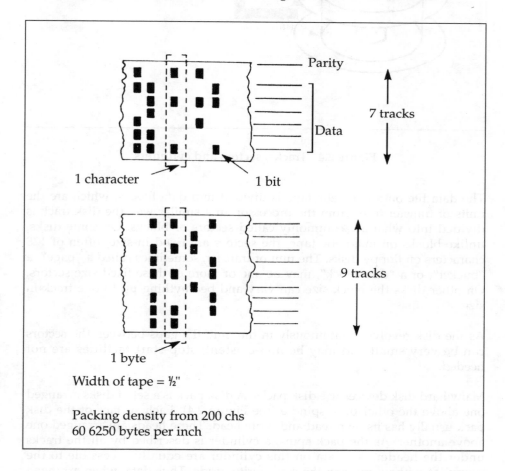

Figure 2.3 Character coding on magnetic tape

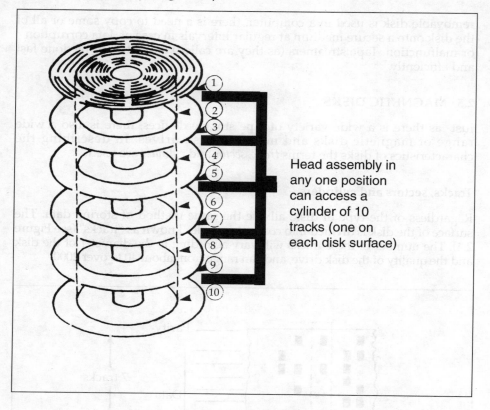

Head assembly in any one position can access a cylinder of 10 tracks (one on each disk surface)

Figure 2.4   Tracks, sectors and cylinders

The data file on a magnetic tape is divided into data blocks, which are the units of transfer to or from the processor. In a similar way the disk track is divided into what are commonly called sectors or blocks. On some disks, unlike blocks on magnetic tape, the sectors are fixed in size, often of 128 characters on floppy disks. The unit of transfer, sometimes called a "page", a "bucket", or a "data block", may be one or more of these fixed size sectors. On other disks the block size can vary and be anything up to one track in size.

As the disk revolves continuously in the unit, the gaps between the sectors can be very small and may be non-existent; stop-start facilities are not needed.

Many hard disk devices use disk packs. A disk pack is a set of disks arranged one above the other on a spindle (see Figure 2.4). Each surface of the disk pack usually has its own read and write head. These heads are arranged one above another. As the pack spins, a cylinder is described by all the tracks under the header. All data on this cylinder are equally accessible to the computer without moving the read/write heads. Thus data, when arranged on disks, are organised into cylinders to reduce access time.

Types of disk

The various disk units fall into two main categories: those that allow a disk or disk-pack or a cartridge to be removed and those that do not. The former are called exchangeable disk drives whereas the latter are called fixed disk drives. There are other types including some that use fixed and exchangeable drives in the same unit.

Disks may also be either rigid or flexible. Rigid (hard) disks may be fixed or removable. Mainframe computer systems commonly use hard disks in removable disk packs (14" diameter is a standard, though other diameters are used) and may have up to 12 disks in the pack (22 useable surfaces, since the top and bottom surfaces in a disk-pack are not used). Some removable disk-packs have the heads sealed into a dust-proof container with the disks, known as a "Winchester".

On small computers, the hard disk sizes tend to be 8", 5¼", or 3½" diameter, and most are sealed Winchester drives. Each hard disk is usually a single disk with both upper and lower surfaces used. Most small computer hard disks are fixed, but there are now disk drives for small computers which allow the Winchester unit to be removed and replaced at will, increasing the amount of data which can be accessed.

Flexible disks ("Floppy" disks or "diskettes") are removable, are mostly used on both sides, and are partially enclosed in a tough plastic sleeve or case. They are available in the same three standard diameters as the hard disks, and there are also 3¼", 3" and 2" versions, but these are less common. Packing densities and number of tracks per surface vary. 48, 96 and 135 tracks per inch are common standards, and capacities include 180 Kb up to 1.6 Mb.

Direct access
The main reason why magnetic disks are more popular in computer systems than magnetic tape, even though tape and tape drives are usually cheaper, is the speed with which information may be retrieved from the disk. To access a data item, the read/write head must be directed to a particular track and then to the appropriate record within that track.

The disks, once in the drive, are spinning continuously, often at thousands of revolutions per minute. The read/write heads are capable of crossing the disk surface from track to track very quickly so a data file, or even a page in the file containing a given record, may be reached in milli-seconds. Thus the disk and its drive give the computer user "direct access" not only to files on the disk but to particular items of data within those files. In contrast, if the information were stored on magnetic tape, many hundreds of feet (metres) of tape might need to be wound on before a particular record could be reached — this is a much slower process.

The table below (Figure 2.5) shows a comparison of some disk devices, with their capacities and costs. Because of the rapid development in this area these figures are likely to change quickly.

Disk drive	3½ floppy	5¼ floppy	3½ hard	Exchange-	Fixed
Typical capacity	0.72 Mb	0.36 Mb	32 Mb	80 Mb	500 Mb
Approximate cost of drive	£100	£115	£150	£1000	£2000+
Approximate cost of disk	80p	35p	integral	£600	integral

Figure 2.5   Disk capacities and prices (1990)

A servo-control mechanism is sometimes used to help position the heads very precisely. This is achieved using a read only head and a pre-recorded track on one surface of the disk pack. The greater precision thus achieved allows the tracks on the other surfaces to be recorded closer together, thus increasing the disk capacity.

Figure 2.6 shows how the costs of using disk storage has decreased rapidly from the 1960s through to 1990.

2.6   OTHER TYPES OF STORAGE

At present, development work is being carried out on magnetic tape and magnetic disks, both to reduce the cost of units and increase their capacity and speed of access. There are also attempts to replace these mechanical devices by solid state units with no moving parts.

Chips

The memory chips used by the CPU are not suitable for backing storage because, once their electric power is removed, they lose the information they contained. However, there is considerable research work being undertaken on memory chips which require very little power so their contents may be retained by using long-life batteries. A number of small computers use this kind of backing store.

Bubble memory

Another solid state device is known as *bubble memory*. This uses the presence or absence of electronic "bubbles" in the device to register binary patterns. These bubbles remain even after electric power is removed and so do not have the drawbacks of conventional memory. Despite the extensive research that has gone into these devices, they have proved very difficult to manufacture successfully and the volume production which would make them cheaper and more readily available is not yet possible.

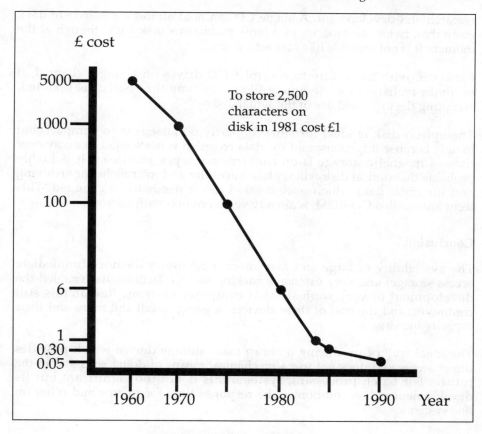

To store 2,500
characters on
disk in 1981 cost £1

Figure 2.6   Disk storage costs

Charge coupled devices

Charge coupled devices are semiconductor devices, which can store small electrical charges to represent bits (in many ways analogous) to magnetic bubbles. Their advantage over magnetic bubbles is faster access time; the disadvantage is that they need a permanent power source to retain data. This may be supplied by battery when the main power is off.

Electron beam memory

Electron beam memory uses an electron beam (as in a cathode ray tube) to store electric charges on a semiconductor device. It is expensive, but possibly has a potential storage capacity greater than large disks, without mechanical movement.

Optical disk

The optical disk, either in its original large video disk form or as the more common compact disk (looking exactly like the audio CD) is another area of research and development. A single CD can hold almost a gigabyte of data, more than twice the capacity of a large mainframe disk pack, though at the moment it is not erasable like magnetic storage.

However, with the ability to control 8 CD drives on a single channel, it becomes realistic to write a new file every time the content is updated, accepting the increased use of the actual disks.

The optical disk is ideal for storage, partly because it is so compact, but mainly because it is robust and the data recorded is not subject to decay over time as magnetic storage is on conventional tapes and disks. It is highly probable that optical disk will replace microfilm and microfiche for archiving and for static data which once created never needs to be changed. This technique, called CD-ROM, is already very common with micros.

Conclusion

The availability of large and fast internal computer memory (immediate access storage) and very extensive backing storage facilities has enabled the development of very sophisticated computer systems. Research is still continuing and the cost of these devices is going to fall still more and their capacity increase.

The ideal way of producing a cheap mass storage device which provides direct access and does not use a mechanical means of doing so is still in the future. For batch processing systems this is not too significant but its development will revolutionise the response time for micros and other on line systems.

NOW TRY THESE...

1. Draw a diagram showing how a magnetic disk is organised into blocks, tracks and cylinders:

    (a) What is the purpose of organising the disk in blocks?

    (b) If the file stored on a moving head disk extends over more than one track why might it be better to store the next part of the file on the same track of another surface rather than on a different track of the same surface?

2. An IT alternative to paper storage of information involves microform. Compare this to paper and electronic storage.

3. Write a brief account of the three levels of computer data storage.

4. Use the data for a typical magnetic tape to answer these questions:

    (a) What is the mean data storage density (bytes per millimetre)?

    (b) What is the proportion of data blocks to inter-block gaps?

(c) What are the maximum and mean data transfer rates?

(d) How long would it take to scan through a whole tape?

5. Sketch a floppy disk and its protective case; outline the functions of the various parts. Compare a floppy disk with a mainframe disk pack.

2.7 INPUT AND OUTPUT

The interface between the computer and the outside world (in particular, the user or operator) is through input and output units. A good human/computer interface makes the implementation and running of new systems much smoother.

It is essential that the right devices are selected, because these are the link between the users and the system itself. Whereas there is a limit to the basic types of computer to choose from, a considerable number of different devices can be connected.

As computer systems have developed from off-line batch processing through multi-access and time-sharing to on-line, real-time systems, so input and output devices have developed in parallel.

Any review of input and output devices cannot be restricted to commercial information technology applications. Industrial control and monitoring computer systems rely heavily upon their physical connection to the processes themselves, reading in representative values of a variety of physical measures and sending out signals which change the operating condition of the plant.

We now look at a wide variety of such devices, giving their advantages and disadvantages, and some examples of the types of application in which they can be used.

The first devices to be considered allow only batch input, and permit no interactive processing. Batch input may be defined as input prepared on specialised machinery and submitted subsequently to the main computer in bulk or batches.

Punched card and paper tape were used as the input/output medium of the early computers. They are still with us today, although in a much reduced capacity. Examples you may know are the Kimball tags used in some clothing shops (see Figure 2.11) and the key cards that open hotel room doors.

2.8 REMOTE BATCH TERMINALS

Remote batch terminals (RBTs) are designed for efficient and reliable transmission of data between the terminal and the computer. Some RBTs are also used for off-line transmission of batches of data to and from similar terminals.

The original specification of an RBT, also known as a Remote Job Entry (RJE) terminal, included a requirement for buffer storage (of some type), a controller (often hard-wired) and a high speed link to the host mainframe computer. The purpose of the RBT was to provide a "transparent" link to a main computer so that the host computer's batch input and output facilities were available locally.

An RBT may now be described as a computer (ie with input, output and processor) that can transfer data to and from a usually more powerful host processor. Thus, many minicomputers will either be supplied in standard systems as remote batch terminals, or have the capability to be used in RBT systems and are very often supplied with that purpose in mind. Similarly, most small business computers will have data transmission facilities to link to large processors if necessary, and most small mainframe computers will have the facilities to link to larger mainframe computers.

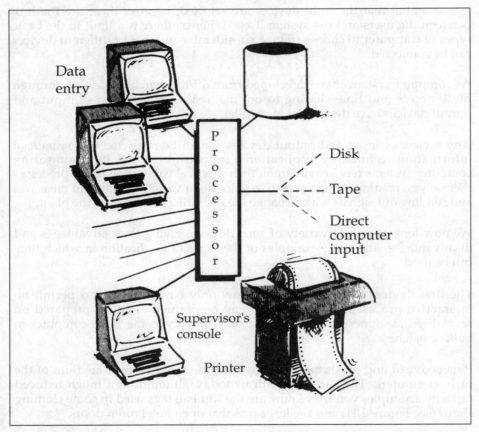

Figure 2.7   Key to store system

The advent of the low-cost network has given a whole range of computers from the smallest micro upwards the capability of operating as a terminal. Local area networks (LANs) are common in buildings where shared storage or peripherals, or simply interaction between terminals, are desirable. Connection to national networks is now also commonplace, for example, a small micro can act as a terminal to a (tightly controlled) system on a bank mainframe for most banking transactions, and large fail-safe computer sites can be linked to others across the world with huge volumes of data transfer ensuring that the integrity of each information technology function is maintained under all foreseeable circumstances.

The next logical development is the key to disk or key to tape system. The operators use keyboards connected to a processor which output the data onto a reel of magnetic tape or a disk. Provision is made to allow the operator to see the last few characters typed. At the appropriate time the data is input to the main computer, either by direct transfer or by transportation of a tape or removable disk pack (see Figure 2.7).

The main purposes of such systems are:

— to improve the quality of data preparation, ie to produce input data with fewer errors

— to reduce the load on the main computer.

The improvement in the quality of the data preparation is achieved by validation, which takes two forms. The first is "field" validation which checks that, for example, alphabetic characters are not wrongly punched into numeric fields or that the value of the field does not lie outside its permitted values. The second kind of validation checks the relationship between fields the presence or absence of one field depending on the value of another, or the totalling of fields to check against control values.

This method of input to the main computer means that data can be read at very high speed, with the majority of errors already eliminated from the input data. This results in a more efficient overall system.

Further benefits accrue from the use of the key to store system, such as the central processor being able to produce management statistics on operator performance. These details may be accessed by the supervisor's console which is allowed to perform these "privileged" tasks.

2.9 INTERACTIVE DEVICES

Interactive devices may be described as those linking the user directly with the computer. This linkage represents major advantages but also means that the selection of suitable devices is crucial to the success or failure of the system. The keyboard with a visual display unit (VDU) is an example of an input/output device which allow a response to be sent by the computer to the point at which the data originated. This is a "conversational" mode, giving immediate acknowledgement to the user, together with prompts and comments on any errors.

The devices are often called terminals, since in medium and large scale computer systems they may be situated at locations remote from the CPU, although the operators may also interact with the system via local connections.

In small computer systems, such as minis and micros, the VDU is often local to (and sometimes integral with) the processor. Some terminals are designed to send data only, but not to receive data; the converse is true of other terminals.

Manufacturers will often supply both a local and remote version of a particular model of terminal. If a terminal is to be connected to a computer in the same building, it may be possible to connect them by means of a cable rather than a circuit supplied by the telephone authority. In this case a terminal is said to be locally connected to the computer. On the other hand, if the terminal is connected to the computer via an external circuit, the terminal is said to be connected remotely.

Figure 2.8   Visual display unit

Thus a terminal is described as local or remote depending on its method of connection to a computer.

Visual Display Units (VDUs)

The VDU (Figure 2.8) is a keyboard terminal. It is designed for interactive applications, but uses a Cathode Ray Tube (CRT) instead of a printer to display input and output messages. This type of terminal benefits the user who requires increased speed, silence and convenience but who does not necessarily need hard-copy records of messages received and sent. A small dot matrix or inkjet printer is often used with a VDU to provide a hard-copy facility.

A VDU consists of a keyboard for manual input of characters and a screen which displays the characters held at the terminal's character store. Electronic circuits control the display of the characters, the editing of data held in the store and the interface between the terminal and the transmission line. A VDU which has all these components in one self-contained unit is called a stand-alone terminal.

In some cases where a group of VDUs is required, it is often cheaper not to use "stand-alone" models, but to use models specially designed for use in clusters sometimes called display stations or display systems. These display stations consist only of a keyboard and display screen. They are attached to a controller which contains the memory logic circuits to support several display stations.

There are two methods of transmission. In the first, each character is transmitted to the computer as it is entered. In the second, the characters are keyed into the memory of the VDU and then, on depression of the "end of message" (send; transmit) key, the entire contents of memory, or selected parts, are transmitted to the computer. This allows several VDUs to share a single transmission line efficiently.

Input features

The keyboards of these terminals are typically like that shown in Figure 2.9 with a ten key numeric pad frequently included or optionally available. Special keys are supplied for moving the cursor about the screen. The cursor is the symbol displayed on the screen at the position where the next character to be keyed in will be entered, or where an existing character is to be deleted or altered. In addition to the cursor movement keys, others are usually provided to assist in editing and formatting, eg tabbing horizontally and vertically, insertion and deletion of characters and lines are common facilities.

Function keys are either numbered as shown, or, for dedicated applications such as word processing, may have keytops describing the function. The function keys are programmed by the software currently loaded into the terminal or micro, and thus will have different meanings when different tasks are being performed.

On many models it is possible to display a form on the screen using a protected field format. The operator cannot key data inside the protected areas, which are enclosed by special characters. The operator enters data in the open or unprotected fields. When the complete message has been composed and checked visually only the variable data is sent to the computer. This is sometimes called "partial transmission" and can reduce the load on the transmission line substantially, as the fixed headings and blank spaces on the screen (except for those in the variable fields) are not transmitted.

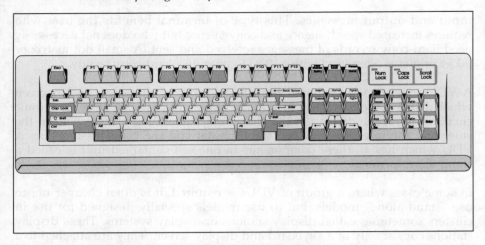

Figure 2.9   A typical VDU keyboard

Output features

Screen size varies considerably, but may be typically 8 inches high by 10 inches wide providing 40 or 80 characters per line and 20 to 25 lines in length.

For a 2000 character display, there is also considerable variety in the format and size of displayed characters, eg a typical character may be 0.1 inches wide and 0.2 inches high.

A brightness and contrast control are usually provided to enable the operator to adjust the image intensity. A blinking (flashing) field facility is available on some terminals which can be used to draw the user's attention to a field. Other terminals offer a different image intensity, a reverse negative effect, or a different character font to identify selected fields. The colours offered vary according to supplier — common ones are green/black, orange/brown and white/black.

Full colour screens — or "monitors" — are becoming widely available and can enhance simple text presentation as well as offering pictorial facilities. As software is developed which uses the colour facility, problems can emerge if the software is run on a monochrome monitor. For example, a deep blue screen with white text, and with a highlight bar in pale blue, with the lettering in bright yellow may look superb, in colour — but the pale blue and yellow may look almost the same on a monochrome screen, and be unreadable.

Many monitors now offer graphical capability with varying degrees of resolution (dots per inch). This can range from the simple 7 x 9 dots per character, giving about 60 dots per inch, to graphics screens giving 300 or many more dots per inch. Each dot "pixel" can be individually addressed, and may have 256 or more colours or shades of grey.

For both locally and remotely connected VDUs, systems can be designed in which several terminals share certain resources.

Several stand-alone VDUs may be connected to a device called a fan out unit (line sharing adaptor or expansion unit) which is situated close to the terminals. Using such an arrangement, remotely connected terminals only need one external circuit and modem.

Many terminals now have a processor or microprocessor built in. Typically, such terminals have the program loaded by the manufacturer and it is resident in read only memory (ROM). Other terminals are programmable by the user or receive downloaded information from the host computer.

2.10 SPECIALISED TERMINALS

Many terminals are designed for use in particular fields of application such as retailing, production control, banking and computer-aided design. This is necessary since the general purpose terminals described earlier cannot meet all the particular requirements of a given application in certain aspects, for example:

— ease of operation by infrequent users or staff with minimal training

— unusual input data requiring specialised keywords

— high throughput with minimum number of key depressions per entry.

These requirements may be met by designing the keyboard so that it contains keys which have specific meanings. Another solution is to have special input devices or readers connected to the terminal. This section gives some examples of such terminals and special input devices.

Point of sale (POS) terminals

These terminals are used in retail or wholesale organisations as the customer transaction occurs. The keyboard may consist of a numeric cluster and some specially labelled keys. These are used to indicate particular types of input, such as method of payment, quantity purchased etc. The terminal may also control one or more of the following specialised input devices:

— bar code reader, either a hand-held device or one built into the counter top for reading bar codes direct from merchandise

— character reader, usually hand-held, for reading specially printed characters on packaging or labels

— a credit card reader

— Kimball tag reader.

Bar-codes are now common. In many countries, it is almost impossible to buy any product, from bread to brake shoes, without noting that the wrapper bears a unique identifier in the form of a bar-code. The code is read by a scanner which transmits a laser beam and receives the reflection from the label. The thickness of the bars and their relative spacing provides a meaningful code.

Plastic credit cards with embossed characters are widely used as a means of

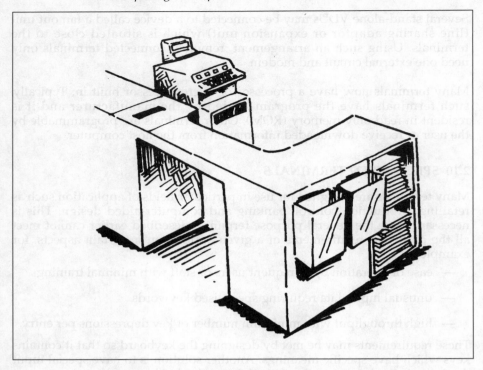

Figure 2.10   Point of sale terminal

identification. These cards have a strip of magnetic tape on them containing coded information. Inserting the card into a slot allows the details to be "read". The use of these cards is often combined with an extra numeric input for greater security. Other uses include "clocking-on", banking terminals and security access.

The Kimball tag (see Figure 2.11) is in effect a miniature punched card containing details of the goods to which it is attached. The tag is removed upon sale of the goods and is read by the point of sale terminal. This method removes any possibility of transcription errors and speeds up operations at the point of sale.

Factory terminal

These terminals are fairly simple rugged devices for collecting information from the shop floor. They have to operate in conditions which at times may be very dirty, hot, noisy and contaminated with various substances.

Operators may not be used to working with keyboards and may be wearing protective gloves. The terminals are often equipped with function keys, levers, rotary switches or buttons for entering variable data with badge readers and card readers for fixed data. Data entered may signal clocking-on or off, or start and finish times or perhaps quantity produced on a certain operation.

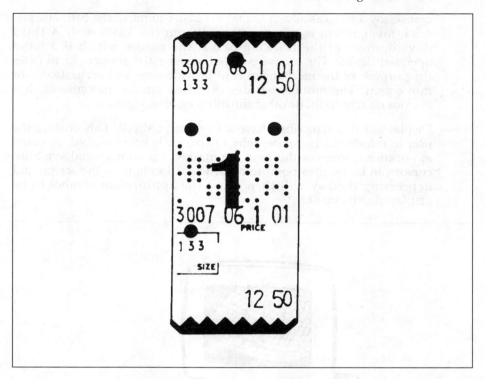

Figure 2.11   A Kimball Tag

Most of the systems were originally designed to be run in an off-line mode with a central recording station which punched the messages either onto paper or cards. Most of today's models, however, can be connected directly to the computer. The computer can either handle the line control and store the message on disk or magnetic tape for later processing, or process the messages as they are received. Similar terminals are found on CNC (computer numerical control) machine tools.

Graphics terminals

There are two basic types of graphics terminals with low or high resolution.

Low resolution graphics can be used in business applications to display graphs, histograms or simple diagrams. High resolution graphics are necessary for applications such as computer-aided design. The devices used to enter graphical information are as follows:

— The light pen, which is a stylus connected by a cable to the terminal. It can be touched to the CRT screen where it can detect the flying spot or raster on the screen as it passes. The computer can detect accurately the position of the light pen. It can, therefore, be used to point to symbols on the screen or to draw lines or figures.

— The tracking ball. The original tracking ball was built into the VDU keyboard and could be moved by running a hand over it. In some cases a joy-stick was added to make it easier to move the ball. The joy-stick mechanism is often separate from the keyboard. A third development of the tracking ball is the mouse which is a hand operated device. The mouse is rolled across a flat surface. In all cases the purpose of the mechanism is to provide easy and accurate cursor movement. The mouse, besides directing cursor movements, has buttons on it to facilitate other functions eg entering data.

— Displays of this type often have a keyboard as well. This enables the user to inform the computer why the cursor is being moved. In many applications, some of the keys are marked up with special symbols; cursor can be used to point to a particular location on the screen and depressing the key will then cause the appropriate symbol to be displayed at this point.

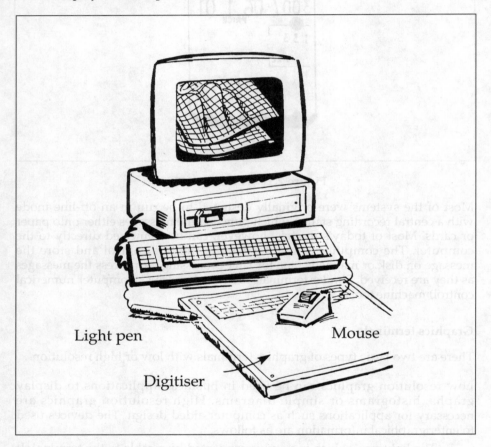

Figure 2.12 Graphics terminal

— The digitiser. This looks similar to a drawing board on which any illustration or drawing can be placed, and then a scanning head (usually called a "puck") is moved to a desired position and a button pressed. This transmits the co-ordinates of the puck position to the system, allowing essentially "analogue" information to be input to the system digitally. Some allow the puck movement to create a string of co-ordinates ("drawing a line") if that option is chosen.

Information once entered is stored by the computer; quite often this implies a three dimensional description of a number of objects which may be displayed from different angles. The components may be built into structures which in turn may be displayed. This facility is being increasingly used in architects' offices to store details of building components such as doors and window frames for use in computer produced plans.

Cash receipting terminals

Another type of terminal is used by public utilities, banks, building societies and local authorities for transactions involving payments into an account and the maintenance of a user book. These cash receipting terminals may also be

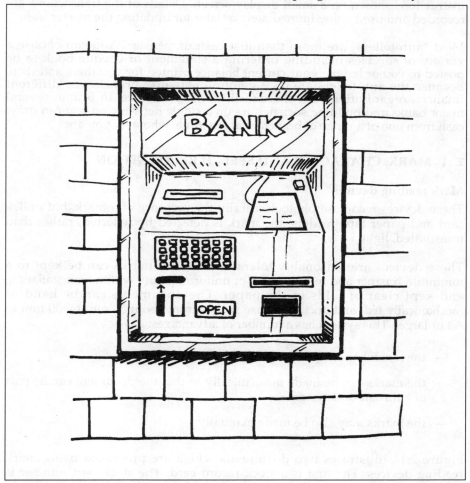

Figure 2.13   Cash dispenser

used for on-line enquiry on an individual account. The terminal has a document chute into which the rent book or pass book is placed. The documents are automatically aligned so that information entered by the clerk is printed on the correct line. The individual's account is also updated. Should the terminal be unable to be used on-line at any time, it can continue to be employed in off-line mode as an automatic cash receipting unit. Details of transactions are printed locally on an audit role and re-keyed later when normal operation is restored; some terminals have the capacity to store a number of transactions so that no re-keying is needed.

Cash dispensers

Cash dispensers (Figure 2.13) are a familiar sight in many towns. A plastic embossed card with information encoded on a magnetic strip is inserted into a slot and a security number input on a small numeric keypad, together with the amount required to be withdrawn. The whole transaction is prompted by instructions shown on a small display screen. Details of the transactions are recorded and used either immediately or later for updating the master files.

Most "autotellers" are more than just cash dispensers. You can choose a variety of services including ordering a statement or cheque book to be posted to you or having your current balance printed for you there and then. Because the autotellers are on a genuine network, branches of different financial organisations can share facilities. For instance, in Britain several major banks and building societies are on a single network, so you can draw cash from one of a range of branches, at any time, wherever you are.

2.11   MARK, CHARACTER AND SPEECH RECOGNITION

Mark reading devices

These devices recognise photoelectrically the presence of a mark, but unlike card and paper tape readers, the mark is detected by reflected, rather than transmitted, light.

These devices are reasonably tolerant. Doubtful marks can be kept to a minimum if paper and markings are of uniform quality within an installation, and kept clear of folds in the paper. The documents can be hand or mechanically fed, and document size ranges from about 50 mm by 30 mm to A4 or larger. This system has a number of advantages:

— the sensing mechanism is fairly cheap

— the marks can be made mechanically so that the document can be part of a turnaround system

— the marks may also be made manually

Figure 2.14 illustrates two documents which are processed using mark reading devices. The first is a stock record card. The stock part number is preprinted on the card and when a stock check is made the stock quantity is entered as marks in the appropriate place on the card. The second example is an answer sheet for a multiple choice question paper. The student simply

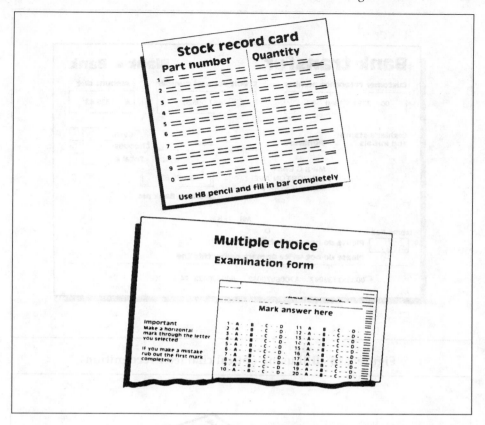

Figure 2.14 Mark read documents

marks his answers as bars through the appropriate entries on the answer sheet.

Optical character recognition (OCR)

Optical systems have now developed to the point at which different shapes of mark, in fact complete sets of alphanumeric characters, can be recognised. Such devices are called OCR devices. Most of these will recognise machine printed characters in a single selected typeface or "font" although some are switchable between "fonts".

This method of input is ideally suited to documents which can be used as turnaround documents. Gas and electricity bills are good examples. The bills are printed with all the information necessary for re-input to the system in an OCR font. If the customer pays the amount stated on the bill then the portion of the bill with the OCR data on it can be returned for direct input to the system. Figure 2.15 shows a typical bill.

The principles have been extended and can now accommodate careful hand printing but not script. This equipment overcomes some of the limitations of mark recognition but at an increased price.

Bank transfer

Blank ● Bank

Customer reference number

00 3351 1380 97

Credit account number

7657 00620

Amount due

£   336.43

Cashier's stamp and initials

Signature

Date

Cash

Cheques

Total £

MR B G EAST
262 NORTON AVE.
MANCHESTER 8

82-00-62

Blank ● Bank plc

M8 7FB

D

Items Fee

Please do not fold this counterfoil

3

Please do not write or mark below this line.

003351138097   A7006570062   000336432 74   X

Figure 2.15   Bill using optical character recognition

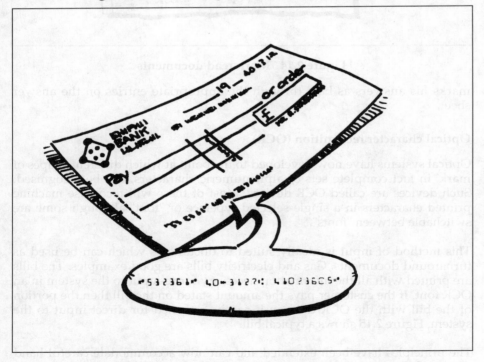

Figure 2.16   MICR characters on a cheque

Magnetic ink character recognition (MICR)

In these systems characters are printed in an ink which can be magnetised so that, after being subjected to a magnetic field, they can be read and decoded. The first major use of MICR was in the banks in the United States, where a font called E13B was adopted. The system was subsequently imported into the United Kingdom banks where it remains the only commercial exploitation of E13B in the country (see Figure 2.16). The MICR readers used by the banks can also sort cheques. An alternative font, CMC7, is widely used in Europe and in the United Kingdom examples of its use can be seen on Postal Orders and Luncheon Vouchers.

The reading station is used to sense and identify the magnetic characters as they pass through. When the characters enter the reading station they are magnetised by the write head. As the magnetised characters pass the reading head, they induce electrical signals in it that are used to identify the characters. Because each character has a rigidly defined shape, the signals produced in the read head are unique and can be easily coded into a form suitable for transmission to the computer.

Documents containing magnetic ink characters can be read at speeds of up to 2,000 6-inch documents per minute. The amount of information that can be contained on each document is limited and it can only be located in special pre-determined positions.

Handwriting recognition

Computer understanding of handwriting and voice input present similar problems; in neither case have the difficulties been completely overcome. People

Figure 2.17 Input tablet

have different handwriting characteristics, just as they have different speech patterns. It is easier to understand individual characters written in isolation than joined-up continuous handwriting.

The early handwriting input devices concentrated on recognising individual characters written in block capital letters only. The use of special pads, which analyse the pressures placed on them by a pen or pencil to interpret what is being written (see Figure 2.17) has increased the reliability and acceptability of handwritten input.

Some handwriting recognition techniques rely on using special pens which register the writing movement. Signatures, for example, can be uniquely identified by the changes in direction and accelerations and decelerations in the speed of a person's writing.

As with speech recognition, the use of handwriting input is likely to be widely used within special well-defined contexts, such as recording standard information on standard forms or in signature verification. Handwriting input could also be used to store and send messages without the computer having to understand what the message says, in a similar way to voicegrams. The output, however, of a handwritten message would probably be on a visual display or printer than by automated handwriting.

Talking to a computer

Speech is a natural form of communication. Babies quickly learn how to communicate by words and other sounds. Computers, however, find speech much more difficult to understand.

Physically, speech consists of sound waves and each word spoken has a characteristic sound pattern. Early computer voice recognition systems worked by trying to identify these individual patterns.

The person using the voice recognition device had to teach the system to understand his or her voice patterns for particular words. This was done by repeating the same word over and over until the computer had analysed a consistent pattern.

The voice recognition system stores the voice patterns so that when the same word was spoken by the same person, the computer would compare the patterns and select the correct word.

Such a voice recognition system has many limitations. It can understand individual words spoken separately; most talking, however, is in the form of continuous speech with words joined in interlocking patterns. It has to be retained for each new operator and every new word. Also, it has a very limited vocabulary, measured in no more than a few thousand words. Very large amounts of memory are also required to store the voice patterns.

The aim of subsequent developments has been to create speech understanding rather than simply voice recognition systems. Continuous speech recognition and enhanced vocabularies are the next step. Techniques are being developed which enable "consensus" voice patterns to be stored. These can be matched to the patterns spoken by many people.

Techniques of direct voice input are continually improving and may well bypass keyboard input in many activities. This includes input over telephone lines as well as by speaking directly into microphones or special devices.

Voice output is also becoming a useful output method. There are a number of developments in this area. The simplest is recording messages for subsequent output, eg the talking clock and voicegrams. In some developments voice synthesis is being used, eg in the output of numbers.

Note that "voice" is essentially an analogue signal, but computers work with digital signals. One of the first steps in voice recognition is digitising the signal, either by rapid and regular volume and frequency sampling or more complex methods. Some systems which use voice — for example a modern "distress alarm" telephone or answering machine — record the message digitally in a chip, rather than in the more usual analogue form on a tape. There was a period when cars had voice systems built in to warn "low brake fluid" or "fasten safety belt", and these also used digital voice storage, but were not very popular.

Voice input is also being increasingly used in industrial applications, where an operator can continue to use both hands for the work while inputting, say, a part number to the computer.

2.12 SENSORS

For industrial computer applications, such as process control, the computer is required to interact directly with the plant. Since the computer can only communicate with the outside world by using electrical signals, it must conform to certain standards.

The hardware problem is, therefore, to convert the various physical variables to electrical signals, and vice versa. The system requirements are to be able to take appropriate action, depending upon the values read in, and to do this rapidly enough to attain effective control.

Typical physical variables to be presented for input are:

— temperature

— pressure

— flow rate

— light intensity

— electrical voltages in the plant

— electrical currents in the plant

— angular velocity

— switch positions ("on" or "off") .

The conversion from these physical properties to electrical signals is performed by transducers. Signal conditioning and changes in electrical level, to meet the standards of the computer system, is then performed by an interface.

The computer performs output functions by having its electrical signals converted to the required physical functions, eg operating an electrical motor(which in turn could operate a wide variety of equipment) or switching equipment "on" or "off ",

Whilst two-state devices, such as switches, can be represented readily as digital values, with "0" and "1" being equivalent to "off" and "on" respectively, varying quantities present a bigger problem. These varying quantities are usually known as analogue values. These require their interface to contain an analogue-to-digital converter (ADC) for input signals and a digital-to-analogue converter (DAC) for output signals. The processor then reads (or writes) digital values to or from registers corresponding to the particular analogue values of the plant.

2.13 PRINTERS

As far as output is concerned, we have already looked at screens, although flat screen displays are becoming very common. The other main output unit is the printer. We can class printers into four main types:

— character

— line

— graphics (plotter)

— page.

Character printers

In the section on terminals, the use of a printer associated with a keyboard was introduced. Modern character printers have been designed with computers in mind. Although they still print one character at a time, a great deal of ingenuity has gone into improving speed and to reducing the number of moving parts. Additional paper movement has been improved by the application of tractors and paper movement controls. Character printers fall into two groups, solid character printers and dot matrix printers.

Solid characters are like those produced on a typewriter, usually by characters embossed on the radiating spokes of a plastic "daisy wheel" (see Figure 2.18) which travels the width of the paper, rotating until the selected character is in position and then struck by a hammer. Daisy wheel printers usually give a better quality of print but are more expensive than dot matrix printers. Daisy wheel characters can have very fine increments of character and line spacing, and some can be used to draw simple graphics. Printers of this type are available which can either use continuous stationery or single sheet feed.

Dot matrix printers do not have a set of characters embossed or otherwise available to view. They form the characters by building them up by dots, each dot being produced by firing a wire passing through a solenoid at the inked ribbon, paper and platen.

Ink-jet and laser printers are technically non-impact dot-matrix printers, but are usually classed with page printers (see later in this section). Thermal printers use coated paper and transmit a spark which blackens the paper. These are dot matrix printers, are practically silent in use, but are expensive to run and so have only limited applications.

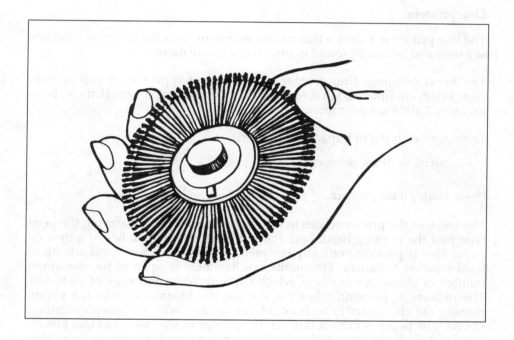

Figure 2.18 Daisy wheel

The simplest dot matrix printers have 9 pins to form the characters (9 pins in a vertical row, a character being made by several impacts, moving progressively across the paper), better ones have 24 pins. Speeds vary from a fairly slow 80 characters per second (cps) to over 500 cps. Most now have microprocessors built in which provide for:

— bi-directional printing

— different fonts

— different densities of printing

— different character sizes.

All dot matrix printers can output graphics, and a few have a multi-colour facility.

Ink-jet

Instead of firing metal pins at the page, through an inked or carbon ribbon, the ink-jet printer combines the ideas of the CRT and the dot matrix. Electrically charged tiny droplets of ink are fired from a nozzle, and they are deflected by electromagnetism (like the electron beam in a CRT) to drop away from the paper or hit it in a precise position. The print is thus built up, a character at a time, at a much higher resolution and higher speed than can be achieved with wire pins. 540 characters per second at a resolution of 300 dpi is not uncommon, but the range is wide.

Line printers

The line printer is a device that produces output from the computer one line at a time and is usually found in mainframe installations.

The most common line printer is the impact type which prints onto sprocketed, continuous, fan-folded, multi-part paper at speeds that can be in excess of 1,500 lines per minute.

There are two types of impact line printer:

— barrel or drum printers

— chain/train printers.

The name of the printer relates to the method employed in carrying the print type past the printing head. Both types of printer print one line at a time on paper that is passing vertically between the barrel or chain, and a bank of fixed-position hammers. The number of hammers is equal to the maximum number of characters in a line, which is normally in the range of 80 to 160. The process of printing takes place when the hammers strike the paper, causing the characters to be brought into contact with it through a carbon ribbon. The paper is moved through the printer in increments of one line by pins located on a tractor or wheel which engages sprocket holes on both sides of the paper. The driving mechanism can be adjusted to accommodate paper widths of up to 18 inches.

On barrel printers the characters are arranged in "rings" around the surface of the drum or barrel, each "ring" containing a complete character set (see Figure 2.19). The barrel rotates continuously; therefore the maximum time taken to print a line is equal to the time taken to complete one revolution. In the case of the chain printer the print characters are mounted on a chain or a belt.

The chain rotates continuously, moving the characters horizontally across a bank of hammers. In a train printer the individual characters are mounted in a track and not fixed to each other; otherwise, they function similarly to a chain printer.

The maximum time taken to print a line is equal to the time taken to pass the complete character set through the hammers.

Because the hammers strike the characters as they are moving, the time the hammer takes to reach the paper has to be compensated for. This is done by firing the hammer before the required character is aligned with the head. Relative variations in the timing of the hammers produce misalignment of printed characters. On the barrel printer this results in an uneven line height, although character spacing will be perfect. On the train printer the effect is to produce uneven character spacing; the line of print will, however, always be perfectly straight. In practice uneven character spacing is more acceptable to the eye and therefore the train printer is considered to give a better quality output. On train printers, print fonts can be changed to suit the application.

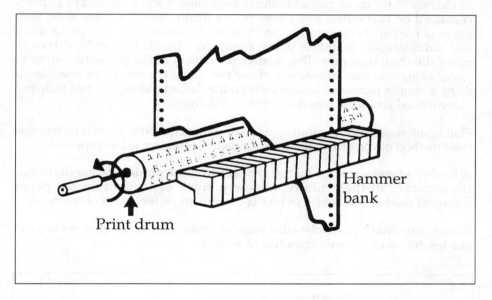

Figure 2.19   Drum printer

After a line has been printed the paper is moved to the next print position. This is referred to as line feed. During this time, the next set of characters is fed from the computer into the printer buffer store to await printing. This is necessary since a complete line of characters must be available before the printing cycle commences.

Graphics printers

The output of graphics using dot matrix and daisy wheel printers has been mentioned. However the resolution of such devices is limited and for high quality diagrams the graph plotter is required.

The graph plotter consists of a pen that can be located, under program control over any point on a sheet of paper. Commands exist to lower or raise the pen, so that any required drawing can be automatically produced. Positioning information is provided by the computer in the form of X/Y co-ordinates. A separate motor controls the movement of the pen along each axis. The unit of movement is an increment; the basic size of an increment can be as small as a few thousandths of an inch.

There are two basic types of plotter:

— flatbed

— drum.

On the flatbed plotters the paper is held on a flat plotting table. The pen is held on an arm set across the paper and an axis motor moves the pen incrementally along the arm. The arm is moved incrementally along the paper by the other axis motor.

In the case of the drum plotter both the paper and the pen move. The paper is contained on two rollers and passes over a drum. Sprocket holes along both edges of the paper engage with sprockets on the drum to provide paper drive and automatically maintain paper alignment. The drum can be driven in either direction thus providing relative movement of the pen with respect to paper along one axis. Movement of the pen along the other axis is achieved using a similar technique to that used on the flatbed plotter; the pen is driven along a fixed arm set across the length of the drum.

Flatbed plotters produce more accurate drawings than the drum type because their method of construction allows a smaller increment to be employed.

A further advantage of the flatbed type is that it can produce larger drawings; the accuracy of the drum type is very much dependent on the paper transport mechanism, which in turn is dependent on the width of the paper.

Plotters can produce complete drawings at a rate of several inches per second at a resolution of a few thousandths of an inch.

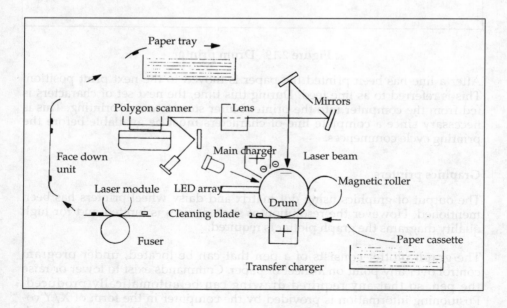

Figure 2.20 Laser printer

Page printers

Modern page printers use the light from a laser or row of light-emitting diodes to project the image of a character onto a drum; then prints in much the same way as a photocopier. The resolution which can be achieved is greater than for any printer we have considered so far, and the output, measured in pages per minute can be from one or two upwards. (A page may be equated to about 3000 characters but can include high quality graphics). The output from a laser printer is usually considered good enough quality to act as a master for publication, but it is still not nearly as good as the true typesetting resolution of 1,500 dpi.

Microfilm

Microfilm is not strictly a computer output medium, but is "printed" as an off-line process. However, as a computer is required to assemble and edit the information and write it onto magnetic tape as part of the COM (computer output on microfilm) process, it is convenient to include it here.

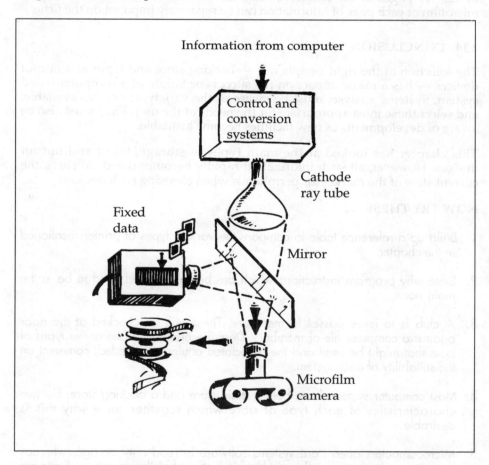

Figure 2.21 Computer output on microfilm

Much commercial computer printed output presents a handling and storage problem, and COM has been developed to help solve this problem.

When the film has been developed it can be stored in a microfilm library until required. A user can access the stored information by placing the film in a standard microfilm reader, which projects an enlarged image onto a screen. Many motor spares organisations now keep their parts catalogues on microfilm, and some building societies use the same medium to record account balances.

A COM recorder (see Figure 2.21) is a device that accepts standard digital information from a computer, transforms it into readable characters and records it onto microfilm at a very high speed — up to half a million characters per second. The use of microfilm provides high-density inexpensive recording and small size for ease of handling and speed of retrieval.

Output can also be made to microfiche. A *microfiche* can contain the equivalent of 128 A4 pages of information. They can be created in the same way as microfilm or each page of information can be separately imposed on the fiche.

2.14 CONCLUSION

The selection of the right peripherals — backing store and input and output devices — has a major impact on the success or failure of a computer-based system. Systems analysts must be aware of the variety of devices available, and select those most appropriate for the needs of the user. They must also be aware of developments as new facilities become available.

This chapter has looked at the main types of storage, input and output devices. However, all such information rapidly becomes dated, so check the current state of the market for peripherals when choosing such devices.

NOW TRY THESE . . .

1. Build up a reference table to compare the various types of printer mentioned in the chapter.

2. State why program instructions which are being executed need to be in the main store.

3. A club is to issue passes to members. These will be checked at the door against a computer file of members. Describe briefly two alternative types of pass that might be used and the associated equipment needed; comment on the suitability of each system.

4. Most computer systems have both a main store and a backing store. List two characteristics of each type of store which together show why this is desirable.

5. Microcomputers often store systems software in read only storage, whereas large computers normally use backing store for the purpose. State an advantage of each method for storing system software.

3 Principles of communication

OBJECTIVES

When you have worked through this chapter, you should be able to:

— outline the principles of communications between computers

— list some uses of electronic data interchange

— state how simplex, half duplex and full duplex transfers differ

— list and comment on the five parts of a data communication system

— compare digital and analogue signals and explain the function of modems

— compare serial and parallel data transfers

— compare bit/s and baud as units of data transfer speed

— state the nature and function of multiplexing and outline two common systems

— compare synchronous and asynchronous transfer

— sketch some types of network architecture and note advantages and disadvantages

— compare local and wide area networking in use and technology.

INTRODUCTION

The development of computer systems has been combined with improved communication facilities which extend the power of the computer beyond the computer room, and allow system benefits to be more widely available. This combination allows computer facilities at remote sites, whilst preserving on one site the expertise needed to operate the whole system. The simplest example is the "dialling-up" on the telephone network to connect a remote terminal with the computer and all its facilities.

Figure 3.1 is an example of a combination of computers and a communications network for a large firm with numerous branch offices and several factories. Each of the factories could have its own medium-sized computer, linked to terminals within the factory and further terminals at adjacent branch offices. Communications links could also exist between these machines and a larger machine at the corporate headquarters. The individual terminals would be used for the collection and dissemination of the user data, with the "satellite" computer collating and editing this data and carrying out much of the total data processing. Major computation and corporate matters would be passed to and handled by the large machine at headquarters.

This blend of computers and communications is now taken for granted. Even the most unsophisticated user may unknowingly be using very complex systems. For example, a small business may have a fairly simple terminal which is connected, via telephone, to a local computer service bureau, in order to use one of the facilities offered by that bureau.

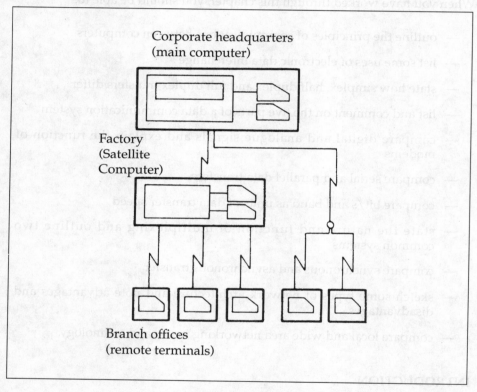

Figure 3.1   Simplified data communication network

Unknown to the user, however, the local call may link to a system a very long way from home (see Figure 3.2). The first connection is to the local small communications computer. This concentrates the data, along with that from other local users, and passes it to a larger computer in the capital. Here, because of the particular services being used, it is passed via a communications satellite in orbit above the ocean, to the service company's main computer centre in the United States. The results come back over the same links, giving the user the impression that the bureau is just next door.

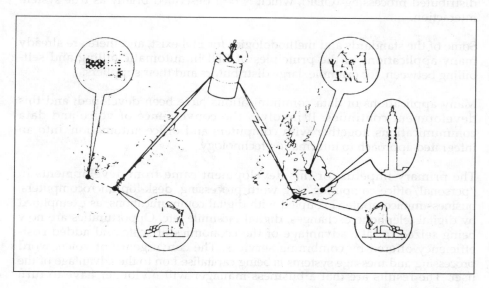

Figure 3.2 International data communications

3.1 ELECTRONIC DATA INTERCHANGE

Alongside the development and convergence of computing and communication technologies has come business needs to interchange data worldwide.

Electronic data interchange (EDI) is the name given to an approach to satisfying this business requirement. It is not a technology, though it makes use of technology. It includes such specific activities as the automatic placement of orders, automatic billing from a supplier to a customer or self-billing by a customer, automatic funds transfer, and a host of other business activities, all without paper or the delays involved in producing, moving and handling paperwork. It implies a growth in understanding between business operations of each other's needs, and can involve radical re-thinking not only of working practices but even of the central activity of the business itself. This has led to a worldwide concern with managemet retraining and "re-engineering".

A number of technologies are needed to support a fully developed EDI, foremost amongst which is open systems interconnection (OSI), a set of standards and procedures which, because of the existence of standards, protocols and data links at lower levels, allow applications at the highest level to operate.

A progression can be seen in the way developments move towards EDI. First, there is simple data communications, allowing data transfer, becoming available through telecommunications development. Next, there is OSI, allowing interworking between systems. The existence of OSI allows open distributed processing (ODP), which is best described briefly as true system interaction.

Some of the standards and methodologies for EDI exist, and there are already many applications of the principles of EDI in automatic billing and self-billing between, for example, large distributors and their suppliers.

Many applications of data communications have been developed, and this development continues. It involves the convergence of voice and data communications, together with computers and office automation, into an integrated approach to information technology.

The primary impetus for this development came from developments in "personal/office computing" (eg word processing, desk-top microcomputers, business minicomputers) coupled with digital communications, as exemplified by digital telephone exchanges, digital facsimile, etc. Opportunities are now being seized to take advantage of the economies of scale and added cost-efficiency offered by combining services. The convergence of voice, word processing and message systems is being capitalised on to the advantage of the user. The results are that a business manager will no longer have to turn separately to:

— the information technology department for computer services

— the PABX for telephones

— the typing pool for document preparation

— a secretary for messages

— the mail room for document transmission.

The technology of telematics in the automated office offers such services as:

— distributed computing

— multi-feature digital telephones

— word processing with remote communications

— voice and electronic mail.

Data communications are used to link the systems both locally and throughout the networks by digital transmission. It is thus possible to transmit information in all its forms with equal facility. The forms include speech, numerical information, text and images, whether in fax or video format.

The essential element, as we have seen, is communication. In the remainder of this chapter, the basic principles will be described and developed to show how communication is achieved at the speeds now available.

3.2 INFORMATION COMMUNICATION

You are part of an information system. I am the message source, or transmitter, the book is the message medium, and you are the receiver. This is "simplex" transmission, one way. In a telephone conversation, messages are transmitted both ways, but not usually simultaneously. This is "half- duplex" transmission, two-way alternately. The poetic descriptions of "people gazing into each other's eyes" and receiving information simultaneously are, of course, describing "duplex" transmission, sometimes called "full duplex" for clarity.

It is only recently that communication itself has been studied. Through the ages, people have tended to concentrate on the methods of communication. Communication theory has provided a better understanding of the factors which limit the rate at which meaningful information can be transferred. To the communications theorist, information is simply 'any organised collection of signals'. This includes sound waves of speech and tones or groups of tones either containing coded information or perhaps music. Collectively, the information makes up the message. Noise is a technical term in communication theory, and means 'any signal which interferes with the message'. Music, however beautiful, could be noise to two people wishing to converse — just as their conversation could be noise to someone wanting to listen to the music.

As well as the "noise" problem, any communication channel has only a finite capacity. This is not a problem in speech conversation, but has implications for information transmission in the general sense. It is important to understand, and have precise definitions for, the concepts, principles and terms used in information communication.

Data transmission

Data transmission is the movement of information using some form of representation appropriate to the transmission medium. This will include:

— electrical signals carried along a conductor

— optical signals along an optical fibre

— electro-magnetic waves, eg radio, or infra-red signals transmitted through space.

Data communications

Data communications includes data transmission, but also includes the control, checking and handling the movement of information. In computer systems, it includes:

— the physical transmission circuits and networks

— the hardware and software which support the data communication functions

— procedures for detecting and recovering from errors

— standards for interfacing user equipment to the network or medium

— rules and protocols to ensure the disciplined (and therefore comprehensible) exchange of information.

Telephone networks

The world telephone networks have been adapted successfully to carry digital data. Although the medium is far from ideal, it has enabled a large number of on-line computer applications to be developed.

The main elements of a telephone system are:

— terminals (typically telephones)

— transmission links

— exchanges

— signalling.

These allow the connection of a telephone on its own exchange to be connected to a telephone in another exchange anywhere in the world. It is the largest and most complex man-made systems there is. At the end of the 1980s, there were about 600 million telephones in over 150 countries worldwide.

Digital vs analogue

An analogue signal is basically a waveform, probably an extremely complex one. The digital signal is basically "on" or "off". To use the analogue network for digital transmission, the solution adopted was to send a "carrier" of a regular waveform, and then use the digital signal to alter (code) the signal. The alterations could then be decoded on receipt, back into the digital form. There are many ways of "modulating" a signal, as we will see in later sections. The basic task of producing the carrier waveform, modulating and then demodulating it, is done by "modems" (MOdulator/DEModulators) at both ends of the transmission link, so that half or full duplex transmission can take place.

In any transmission a pair of modems is used, as illustrated in Figure 3.3.

If a network is built to handle digital data, then this can be used for analogue signalling, by 'sampling' the analogue signal frequently enough to enable its reconstruction in comprehensible form at the recipient end of the transmission.

Throughout the world the communications authorities are moving away from analogue systems in favour of wholly digital transmission facilities. These facilities, when linked with programmed exchanges can handle speech as a digital signal and more importantly can handle the digital output from data terminals.

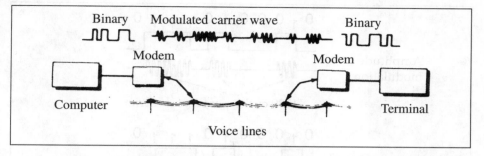

Figure 3.3   The use of modems (after Martin 1967)

The gradual change to digital facilities is under way, but until it is complete, the modem will still be used to convert the digital output of a terminal into a form which is electrically similar to the analogue signals representing speech.

3.3   DATA TRANSMISSION

Parallel vs serial transmission

When data in the form of characters is required to be transmitted from one device to another, there are two possible approaches. Either the bit pattern of the character is transmitted all at once, with a separate wire carrying each of the (say) 8-bits in parallel, or the bits are transmitted serially, one after the other down a single conductor.

Parallel transmission is obviously faster, but requires multi-way cables ("data buses"). Also parallel transmission works over only fairly short distances, within a room or a building, say.

Serial transmission lends itself readily to the use of the existing telephone network because of its single wire design, and this is the data transmission technique used over longer distances.

Modulation

Modulation is the process of electrically altering some property of one signal (the carrier) in relation to another signal (speech or data). See Figure 3.4.

Amplitude modulation (changing the "volume") alters the maximum and minimum extent of a carrier. Normally a continuous carrier is used, allowingbreaks to be detected, but the method suffers badly from noise. In mechanical switching systems, as all telephone switches were originally, every make or break can introduce a pulse into the signal network. Clearly the demodulator does not know whether it was a pulse of data or not. Also, random noise tends to blur the distinction between '0' and '1' states. Amplification does not help a great deal, because the noise gets amplified with the signal. Amplitude modulation is therefore not used by itself, but it illustrates the idea of modulation clearly, and it is used as a component of more advanced methods.

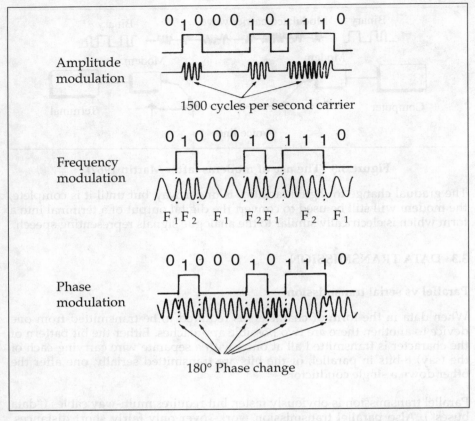

0 1 0 0 0 1 0 1 1 1 0

Amplitude
modulation

1500 cycles per second carrier

0 1 0 0 0 1 0 1 1 1 0

Frequency
modulation

$F_1 F_2$ F_1 $F_2 F_1$ F_2 F_1

0 1 0 0 0 1 0 1 1 1 0

Phase
modulation

180° Phase change

Figure 3.4   Binary signal and modulation forms

Frequency modulation in principle uses two different frequencies for binary 0 and 1. In audio terms, the effect is of two different 'notes' or tones, one higher than the other.

In the modem, a voltage detector simply switches the output signal between the outputs from two frequency generators — the generators run continuously, but the output is from one or the other according to the bit pattern.

This shifting of frequency gives rise to a common short name for frequency modulation — frequency shift keying (FSK). At the receiving end, the demodulator will examine the incoming signal for a match with one of the two frequencies, and will switch the output to the terminal between + 6v and - 6v when it detects the right frequency (within fairly close tolerance) for the necessary signal element duration. Occasional noise, of shorter duration than a signal element, can thus be ignored.

Data transmission speeds

Two terms are used to define the speed of transmission, one referring to information transfer, the other to the signal characteristics of the transmission link. These are 'bits per second' and "baud".

Bits per second is a measure of the rate at which binary data is transmitted. This will include the actual information bits plus control bits and checking bits.

Baud is a measure of the rate at which changes in the signal state occur. This is the number of 'signal elements'.

Often the two terms are used indiscriminately. However, with more advanced signalling, the bits/sec may not be the same as the baud. If a signal state can represent more than one data bit, a faster bits/sec transmission can be achieved at the same baud rate.

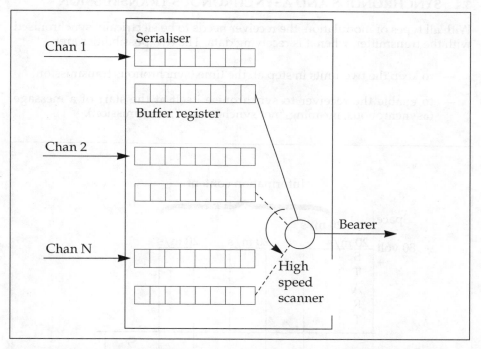

Figure 3.5   Simplified diagram of a character interleaved TDM

Multiplexing

With higher data transmission rates, the capacity can be shared amongst different devices using multiplexing. Each device is connected to a multiplexor which is connected (via a modem) to the line.

Two main approaches are used, frequency division multiplexing (FDM) and time division multiplexing (TDM).

FDM divides the available transmission band into groups of frequencies. For example it is possible to derive 12 channels (each of 240 Hz bandwidth) from an analogue speech line. Although this reduces the per channel costs it is inherently inflexible and offers only low channel bit rates (up to 110 bits/sec).

TDM is a newer technique for data transmission, which requires data storage. (Incidentally, this has long been the technique used in multiplexor channels inside a computer.) Figure 3.5 shows a simplified character interleaved multiplexor with a number of input channels entering data into serialisers and in turn into buffer registers. A high speed scanner samples the register allocated to the low speed input channels taking the contents, (in this case a complete character) and interleaving this with characters from the other registers. A complete scan of all registers termed a "frame" is transmitted over the bearer circuits to the demultiplexor at the distant end.

3.4   SYNCHRONOUS AND ASYNCHRONOUS TRANSMISSION

With all types of modulation, the receiver needs to be electrically synchronised with the transmitter, when it is receiving data. The two possibilities are:

— to keep the two units in step all the time (synchronous transmission)

— to enable the receiver to synchronise itself at the start of a message (asynchronous, meaning "not synchronous", transmission).

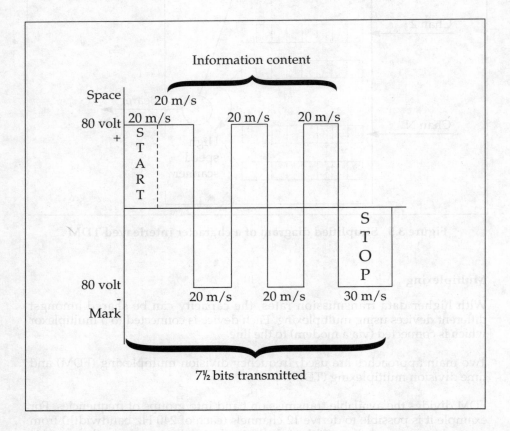

Figure 3.6   Start/Stop asynchronous working (CCITT No.2 Code)

Asynchronous transmission is a simple character based method of keeping the two devices in step when this is needed — when an information signal is being received. The information — the coded representation of a letter or number — is "framed" by additional bits put on by the transmitter.

The first framing bit, which has positive polarity and "wakes up" the receiver, is known as the "start bit". The transmission is often called "start/stop". If the transmission is fairly slow, such as the speed of keying of a human operator, the mechanism for adding and recognising the framing bits is simple. However, not all asynchronous transmission is either slow or simple. In many applications there are quite sophisticated asynchronous terminals.

They would still frame each character with the start and stop bits, and therefore carry quite a high overhead. If the transmission speed approaches the rated capacity of the channel, the overhead (the framing bits) can become significant in slowing down the actual information transfer rate. Figure 3.6 shows the CCITT code 2 framing of a five bit character with two and half startlstop bits. Clearly as the amount of information being handled reaches the capacity of the channel, one third of that capacity is "wasted".

Synchronous transfer is a "bit" oriented method of keeping the receiving terminal in step with the sending terminal. It requires very accurate timing of the bits sent, which is synchronised to by the receiver. The bits are "clocked out" at a constant rate, usually at a speed far higher than a skilled keyboard operator can achieve.

3.5 THE DATA COMMUNICATIONS SYSTEM

So far this chapter has been concerned with principles and underlying transmission technology which support data communication. However, a data communications system in which terminals communicate with computers and computers communicate with computers in order to achieve specific results, comprises much more than the transmission services.

It involves hardware components such as modems and multiplexors, and these components can be connected together in various configurations, networks and physical architectures. But the users' view of the system, when they access files or applications programs, will generally be different from the physical appearance. In other words, the functional architecture also needs to be considered.

Types of network

Networks consist of two or more locations (nodes) which are connected together using communication links. A node may contain any number of communication and computing devices. A number of special terms are used when describing data links and networks; these are described below.

Point-to-point
A point-to-point network is the simplest and is extensively used (see Figure

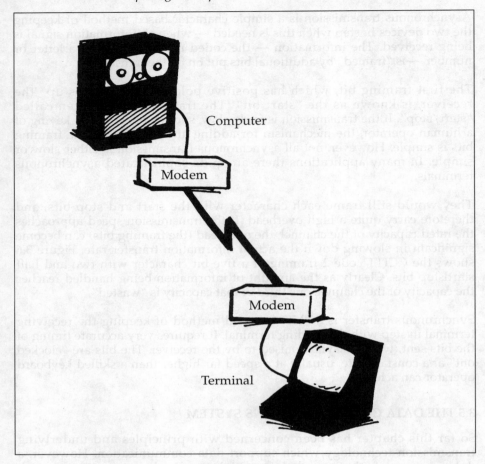

Figure 3.7   Point-to-point data link

3.7). It may be transitory and exist only for the duration of a call as on the switched network, or exist permanently as a leased circuit.

Point-to-point configurations are commonly used where only a limited number of physically distinct routes are involved, and the distances are not excessive.

Multidrop
Where a large number of locations have to be connected, and can be broken down into physical clusters, the multidrop form of configuration is generally more cost-effective (see Figure 3.8).

All transmissions from Node A can be received by Nodes B, C and D. Similarly, only Node A can receive data from B, C and D, only one of which may transmit at a time. Multidrop circuits provide a way of reducing line costs by using a single branched circuit to connect Node A to Nodes B, C and D, rather than the three point-to-point circuits that would otherwise be required. It must be stressed that Nodes B, C and D cannot communicate directly with each other.

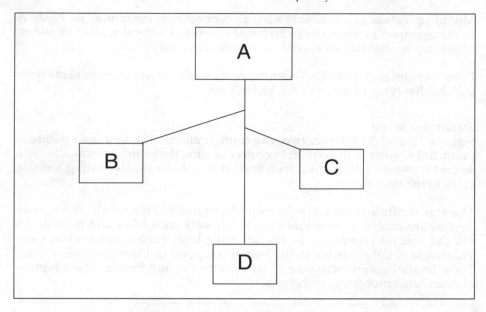

Figure 3.8   Multidrop configuration

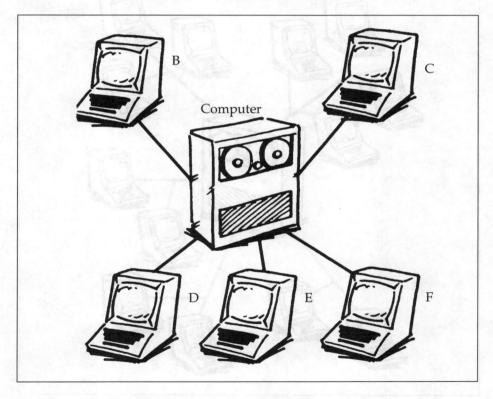

Figure 3.9   Star network using point-to-point circuits

Multidrop networks are mainly used to connect host computers (at Node A in the example) to terminals or terminal clusters at several remote locations. Multidrop configurations are only available on leased circuits.

Point-to-point and multidrop circuits are the basic network components from which other types of network can be built up.

Star configurations

Figures 3.9 and 3.10 depict two star configurations. The first uses point-to-point links, with each terminal connected directly to the central site. The second uses multi-drop links, with several remote terminals sharing a single entry to the central site.

The star configuration has two major limitations. First of all, the remote devices are unable to communicate directly with each other and must do So via the central computer. In the second place, such a network is very vulnerable to failure, either in the central computer or the transmission links. These limitations are overcome in mesh networks and through the adoption of distributed processing principles.

Figure 3.10 Multidropped star network

Loop networks

Loop networks (see Figure 3.11) can be one of two types. In the first, messages are passed from node to node in one direction. In the second, messages are transmitted in both directions so that in the event of one line failure, the host computer can still communicate with all nodes.

Mesh networks

While star networks are suited to linking host computers to slave terminals or computers on a one to many basis, mesh networks are primarily used where multiple hosts need connection to multiple slaves (see Figure 3.12). In many Cases the idea of host and slave is inappropriate as the nodes connected are of equal status.

Mesh networks are very resilient to failure, with alternative data routes being available when data link failure occurs. In many cases this resilience means that users are unaware that a network failure has occurred. Mesh networks are generally very expensive to implement and where circuit lengths are long or data volumes low, a public packet switched service may offer a cost advantage over a private mesh network.

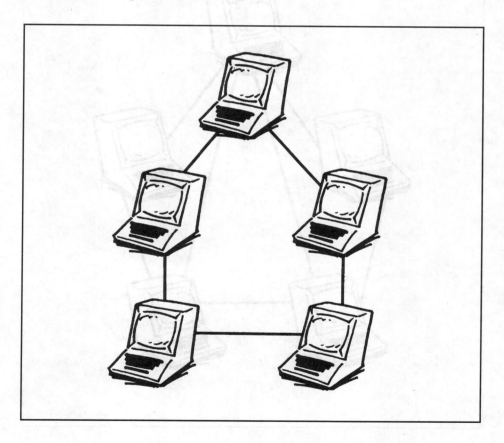

Figure 3.11   A closed-loop network

3.6   WIDE AREA AND LOCAL AREA NETWORKS

The above configurations are used both separately and in combination to build up more extensive networks. These are generally of two types. The first is wide area networks (WAN), which makes use of public phone links and, as the name suggests, must cover a large geographical distance or area, national and international. These are the traditional type of networks used for remote processing and on-line systems. The second, local area networks (LAN), has developed in response to the need to connect many local devices. This requirement has increased greatly with the advent of microcomputers.

Local and wide area networks can be connected together by devices called gateways. These are intelligent devices which are capable of converting the protocols used in one network to those used in the other.

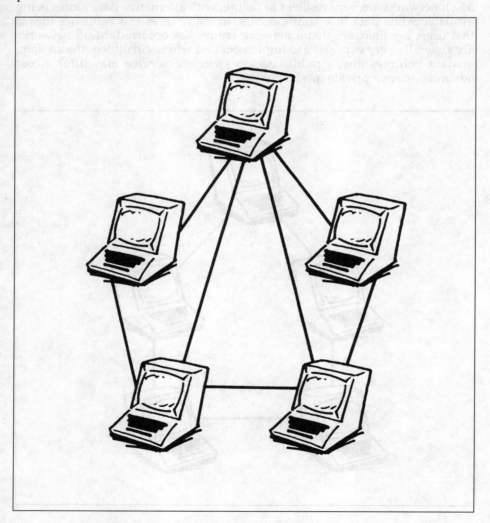

Figure 3.12   Mesh network

Local area networks

The term local area network is applied to networks specifically developed for the interconnection of computers, terminals and other devices at a single geographical site. Being at a single site they are not restricted to the facilities available through the local telephone company. Typically, they will have transmission speeds of up to several megabytes per second. These speeds can be achieved using parallel transmission where a cable with multiple core is used, or serial transmissions, making use of high frequency carriers, using coaxial cables, fibre optics or even a simple pair of wires because distances are short. Modems are not normally required although some mechanism for converting from parallel to serial transmission and back again may be needed.

Two basic transport mechanisms are used in local area networks. The first of these mechanisms is known as "empty slot" or "token passing" and is suited to ring networks. Using the "empty slot" principle, one (or more) data packets circle the network in one direction only, being passed from hand-to-hand between the nodes. When a node needs to send a message, it waits for the arrival of an empty packet and inserts its message, together with the destination node address, into the packet before passing it on to the next node. The destination node takes a copy of the data and marks the packet as having been received but not emptied; the packet completes a revolution of the ring before being "emptied" by the original sender.

The "token passing" principle is very similar in concept. Rather than complete packets (empty and full) permanently circling the ring, only short control messages called tokens are permanently present. Any node wishing to send a message has to await the arrival of a token, then transmits its addressed message followed by the token. Again, the message makes a complete revolution of the ring, being acknowledged by the addressee node as appropriate, before being removed from the network by its originator.

The second mechanism allows nodes to contend for the use of the network using a technique known as "Carrier Sense Multiple Access with Collision Detection" (CSMA/CD). A transmission from any node will be heard by all the others; however, only one node should transmit at a time, as single simultaneous transmission from more than one node could result in collision and data corruption.

Any node wishing to transmit first "listens" to check if another node is already transmitting (whether a carrier signal is present on the network). Once the network is free, the node will transmit its addressed message, but it will continue "listening" to ensure that it is the only node transmitting. In the event that a collision is detected, the node will wait for a random period of time before trying again. The random nature of this delay avoids the possibility that the same two nodes will transmit repeatedly at the same intervals, with each attempt resulting in a collision and neither node ever being able to transmit successfully.

The main attributes of present-day local area networks are:

— inexpensive transmission media

— inexpensive devices to interface to the network

— easy physical connection of devices to the network

— high data transmission rates

— network data transmission rate is independent of the rates used by the attached devices, making it easier for devices of one speed to send information to devices of another speed

— a high degree of interconnection between devices

— every attached device has the potential to communicate with every other device on the network

— a central controlling processor seldom present

— in the majority of cases, each attached device hears (but does not process) messages intended for other devices as well as for itself.

It is important to note that neither the actual data transmission rate used, nor the access method, nor the topology of the network are essential characteristics.

As local area networks have developed, it has become clearer what equipment will use them and what applications will be supported. Although some forms of local area network can be extended to analogue voice equipment (eg the telephone) or to video devices, most are primarily suited to devices generating digital data streams at a moderate rate such as:

— computers (minis, micros, and mainframes)

— computer terminals, both dumb and intelligent

— personal computer systems based on microprocessors

— office workstations

— mass storage devices

— printers and plotters

— file servers

— photo- and teletypesetters

— process monitoring and control equipment

— bridges and gateways to other networks.

The most relevant applications are:

— file transfer and access

— word and text processing

— electronic message handling

— personal filing and information handling

— graphical information

— remote database access

— personal computing

— digital voice transmission and storage.

Special types of local area networks have been developed to link mainframe computer systems which are too far apart to use normal direct wiring, or which are from different suppliers and thus employ different interfaces.

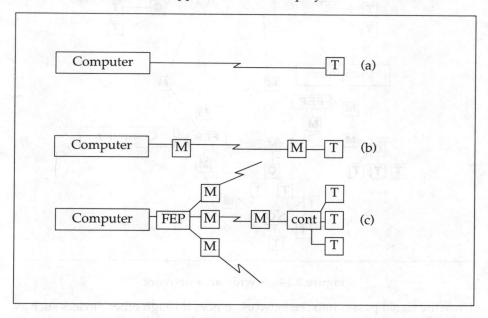

Figure 3.13   Components in a wide area network

Wide area networks

In contrast to local area networks which only have a few components, wide area networks involve a large number of devices between the source and destination of data (normally computer and terminal). Figure 3.13 shows the simplest form of connection in which a terminal is linked directly to the computer. This can be achieved in the local situation but as has been shown, for transmission over any distance it is necessary to insert modems (Figure 3.13). As more lines are needed and because of the special requirements of transmission (the protocols, error checking and correction) communication controllers (often known as front-end processors) have to be introduced. At the other end concentrators are inserted which allow terminals to share the same transmission facility (see Figure 3.13). It also means that any intelligence required could be put in the concentrator thus reducing the cost of terminals.

Front-end processors and concentrators may also be used as nodes on the network or additional devices may be introduced as nodes to facilitate networking (see Figure 3.14).

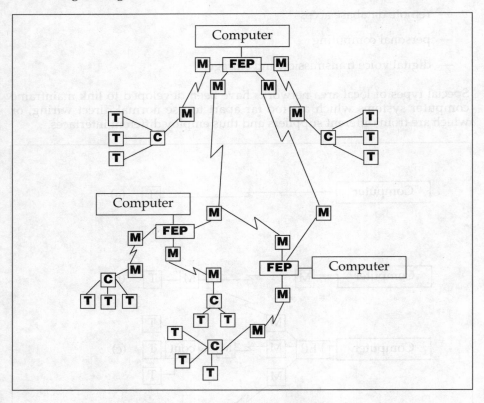

Figure 3.14   A wide area network

Once the signal passes into the network, it goes through other devices such as the exchange equipment. Other modems are also used to boost the signal to higher frequencies and combine it with others for transmission across the network. Transmission can be by coaxial cable or microwave.

Earlier wide area networking used leased lines. However, there are three common approaches to networking which use the PSTN:

— circuit switching

— message switching

— packet switching.

Circuit switching is the normal approach when dial up links are used. It is analogous to a simple telephone call. The line is available for the duration of the call. At the end of a call the circuit is broken and another location can be dialled and a new circuit established. Transmission can only take place once the circuit is established.

With message switching the complete circuit does not have to be established when the message is transmitted. Each message contains within it the address of its destination, in addition to the information to be transmitted.

Each exchange inspects the address of the message's destination, and, providing that an outgoing circuit is free, forwards it on to the next exchange. If there is no outgoing circuit available, or the destination is unable to accept it, the message is stored in a queue of messages, and is subsequently transmitted when circumstances permit. For this reason the method is sometimes known as "store-and-forward" switching.

A message switching system using store-and-forward switching obviates the need for repeated attempts at establishing a call, by accepting the message and undertaking to deliver it when this becomes possible.

Packet switching is similar to message switching except that packets are of a fixed size and carry error checking and, in some cases, error correction information with them. Many messages are broken down into packets for transmission. The advantage over message switching is that the switching nodes can handle the fixed length packets more efficiently and long messages do not block the network.

Both message and packet switching networks also have other advantages over circuit switching:

— Speed matching. The store-and-forward capability enables the behaviour of the equipment and people (mainly the former in this context) involved in an exchange to be more closely matched. The network accepts messages or packets at the rate at which they can be prepared and delivers them at the rate at which the destination can accept them.

— Error retransmission. Each originating point, destination and switching centre can hold a copy of the message or packet so that it can retransmit it in the event of a faulty transmission being signalled. This applies over each component link of the transmission path, whereas using circuit switching it can only be applied end-to-end.

— Alternative routeing. Since each meassge contains its own destination address, all messages can be treated as independent entities so far as the network is concerned. All that matters is that it guarantees to deliver a message or packet to its correct destination irrespective of the actual physical route taken. When more than one distinct physical route exists between two points on the network, this can be turned to an advantage by arranging for the switching centres to select the best alternative in the event of congestion or failure of a circuit.

— Different grades of service. The previous discussion assumed, in effect, that the messages in a queue are released for onward transmission on a first in first-out basis. In fact it is possible to specify different grades of service, so that, for example, messages given a high priority would receive preference over lower priority messages.

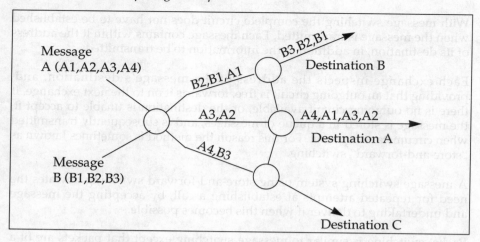

Figure 3.15 Interleaving and multiplexing

— Improved network control opportunities. The presence of computer processing power in the switching exchanges clearly provides opportunities to exercise a level of overall control of the network and its performance.

— End-to-end multiplexing. Because messages and packets are individually addressed and a "call" or interaction between two subscribers does not require a dedicated physical transmission path, it is perfectly legitimate to interleave messages or packets originating and terminating at different addresses (see Figure 3.15).

This has three main consequences:

— It means that the network itself provides multiplexing as an inherent property instead of an add-on facility supplied outside the network through a variety of devices called multiplexors/concentrators.

— Flexible connection/interconnection. Since the network itself helps to match the speed and response characteristics of the communicating parties and their equipment, there is no longer the same requirement for multiple line access ports distinguished by speeds and other transmission characteristics. Traffic originating at different speeds and having different transmission modes (eg synchronous/asynchronous) can share a common access line and port.

— Improved circuit utilisation. Multiplexing within a network clearly results in far higher circuit utilisation than is possible using traditional circuit switching.

NOW TRY THESE . . .

1. Discuss the pros and cons of having your own micro rather than a workstation on a larger system.

2. Compare star (cluster) and ring networks. If your school, college or workplace has one or more networks, sketch the layout(s) and identify the type(s) .

3. Compare such a local area network with other links between computers in your school, college or workplace.

4. Research the pros and cons of the digital phone network over the older analogue system. Write an essay on the subject.

5. Compare your school/college/workplace phone system to a multiuser computer.

   (a) Show, with the aid of a diagram, how a simple microcomputer network can be organised. Explain the purpose of the various parts of the system, and describe and outline how the microcomputers can communicate with each other.

   (b A multi-access system, with several terminals linked to a single computer, is similar to a network in that both allow several users to work at once on the same system. What are the particular advantages of each system?

6. The head office of a bank has ten rooms on each of five floors for office staff involved in maintaining records for all its clients. The society also has 30 branch outlets within a 30 km radius.

   (a) What is meant by the terms LAN and WAN?

   (b) What would be the advantages to the bank of installing a LAN? Where would it be placed?

   (c) What would be the advantages of using a WAN?

   (d) What hardware would give branches on-line access to centrally held data?

7. The bank has recently taken over a smaller one; this is based some 1 00km from the first. It has a similar setup, but with only a small central office and 23 branches. They need to transfer files of several millions of characters between the two head offices each day.

   (e) About how long will it take to transmit a 5 megabyte file at a speed of 9600 bits per second?

   (f) For what purposes would branch offices use on-line access?

8. Study a network; decide what the arrangement used is and what problems that arrangement may cause.

4 Control software and utilities

OBJECTIVES

When you have worked through this chapter, you should be able to:

— list the five main types of software

— compare and explain the nature of multiprogramming and multi-access

— list the main tasks of operating software

— list and briefly explain the main desirable features of operating software

— briefly explain some common tasks of utilities

— outline the main functions of microcomputer operating software

— outline the features of MS-DOS and Unix.

INTRODUCTION

"Software is the part of the computer system (ie programs) which enables the hardware to operate".

This definition, or something very similar, appears in most glossaries of computing terms. However, this chapter and the next are concerned only with software which has been provided by manufacturers, consultants, software houses, or any other outside organisation, and which is written for use by many users.

The software supplied by outside agencies falls into five broad categories:

— operating systems

— utility software

— assemblers and compilers

— programming aids

— application packages.

The first two categories are explained and illustrated in this chapter, whilst Chapter 5 deals with the other three.

4.1 MAINFRAME OPERATING SYSTEMS

An operating system can be regarded as a set of programs which permit the continuous operation of a computer from program to program with the minimum amount of operator intervention; it acts as an interface between the operator, the computer and the processing program.

The American National Standards Institute (ANSI) definition of an operating system is as follows:

> "Software which controls the execution of computer programs and which may provide scheduling, debugging, input/output control, accounting, compilation, storage assignment, data management and related services."

Each of these aspects of an operating system will be discussed in this chapter.

Early systems

In earlier mainframe systems, control programs (a form of simple operating system) were developed which presented a set of operating instructions to the operator. These gave him standard messages concerning the allocation of files to programs, the loading and unloading of magnetic tape units, the beginning and end of a program run, etc. These control programs evolved to a stage at which they could carry out a large number of routine tasks formerly the province of operating staff. When a program failed, for example, it was possible to automatically print (dump) the contents of selected registers and areas of storage, and then continue with the next program. Although the advent of the simple operating system brought considerable improvements in computer throughput, the Central Processing Unit (CPU) was in fact still idle for a large part of the working day. For much of the time, the CPU was waiting for such things as input/output, backing storage searches and tape loading operations. The situation was much improved by the provision of multiprogramming facilities.

Multiprogramming

Multiprogramming is the process of combining hardware and software to create a situation in which more than one program may be held in main store at any one time. Each program has control of the CPU for short periods in an appropriate sequence, in order to achieve optimum utilisation of the CPU and its peripheral devices. The objectives are to minimise unused CPU time, to minimise total elapsed time and to prevent single programs dominating the CPU. To achieve these objectives, the operating system must be able to take control of the CPU from the program currently being executed and pass the control on to another program. This feature prevents one program from dominating the system, it also allows a program that is input/output limited to relinquish control until it has, for example, completed a data transfer.

Multiprogramming is dependent on interrupts. An interrupt provides a means of altering the sequence of instructions being obeyed, and transferring control of subsequent action to the operating system. When control is transferred to the operating system, it is necessary to store information about the status of the current program, to enable that program to be resumed after the interrupt has been serviced. The routine which controls multi-programming usually works to a system of priorities, each program having a level of priority.

For example, if two programs were in the store, one requiring frequent use of the printer but little CPU time, and the other requiring heavy use of the CPU but not the same printer, the first could be given a higher priority than the second. The operating system would allow the first to start printing. As soon as data had been transferred to the printer the program would have to wait for the actual printing to take place so control could be given to the heavy CPU-user program. This could continue until the first program wanted to send another line, and so on. The printer program would thus appear to run at full speed, and the whole of the time the CPU would otherwise have been idle whilst printing was taking place, it would actually be working on the second program. The effect would be that the second program would take only a fraction longer to run than if it had uninterrupted use of the CPU. Two programs would be completed in little more than the time for one running alone.

Using this technique the operating system shares the resources of the computer among a number of programs and attempts to provide an optimum solution for a particular installation's requirements.

4.2 OPERATING SYSTEM FACILITIES

The development of multiprogramming presented complex organisational problems. Some of the many operations required to run each program are:

— program loading

— loading of input data

— loading of files

— allocation of peripherals to the program

— monitoring of the program's actions

— obeying program requests (ie interrupts).

When these factors have to be considered for several programs being run concurrently, there is a need to use the computer's own ability to carry out routine tasks of a complex but precisely defined nature. This is achieved by the operating system, which allocates resources in the most efficient way possible and proceeds to implement the complex requirements with minimal intervention. The facilities offered by operating systems depend on the size of the computer and the particular computer manufacturer. As the number of facilities offered increases, so also does the storage requirement of the operating system. Some operating systems are main store resident, which can be expensive if a comprehensive operating system is employed; others are segmented and overlaid from disc as required, which reduces the main storage requirement at the expense of transfer time overheads. A number of desirable features of comprehensive operating systems are:

— job control language

— failure and recovery

— file security

— logging

— accounting

— scheduling

— operator communication

— multi-access control.

These are now described.

Job control language

Job control language is the means by which the user communicates his requirements to the operating system. It is essential that this language is simple and easy to learn, otherwise the effectiveness of the system will be degraded. In general the user provides a description in job control language of:

— the operating requirements of the job

— likely events during the running of the job

— resulting actions required on the occurrence of such an event.

— the types of statement which can exist in the command language comprise four groups:

— statements concerned with setting up the job, eg peripherals required with correct files loaded

— statements concerned with running the job, eg work space needed for sorting

— statements concerned with connecting software to the system, eg library programs required

— statements available to the user to help control the job, eg built in checkpoints with operator instructions.

In some systems the command language may be supplemented by the use of macro commands (macros), which can be either system or user-defined. System-defined macros provide a powerful and flexible means of interfacing with library software. For example, compiling and running a COBOL program requires numerous command language statements to be used. If, however, these statements are built into a macro it is only necessary for the user or the operator to issue one command to cause all the required operations to be performed. On smaller operating systems, the same function is performed with, for instance, "batch" (.BAT) files. A series of commands in a batch file will be obeyed sequentially, moving to the next as the previous one is completed. User-defined macros or batch files can be used to extend the power of the command language to cater for particular needs. For example all the command language statements necessary for a particular application can be combined and issued as a single command. A well defined, multi-function command language provides an efficient and powerful means by which users and operators may communicate their requirements to the computer. In addition, it will reduce the users' dependence on the operator, and removes ambiguity from the interpretation and execution of instructions. A tested macro or batch file removes the possibility of human error in repeating complex sequences of commands.

Failure and recovery

The operating system handles interrupts which indicate various conditions. For example, the occurrence of an invalid instruction in a program; an attempted access by one program to portions of computer storage reserved for another; the occurrence of an overflow in an area of storage used for arithmetic. On detecting the interrupt the operating system may either halt processing and signal the operator or switch control to user-written error recovery routines.

Since there is always the danger of a computer breaking down in the middle of processing a program, operating systems provide the facilities for periodically "dumping" the contents of critical areas of storage. These "snapshots" of the contents of the immediate access storage (IAS) can be used, in the event of failure, to reconstitute the system to the state it was in at the last dump, making it unnecessary to restart programs from the beginning. In some systems, "checkpoints" can be incorporated by which the user may specify re-starting points within his program. Dumping takes place to tape or disks, and in most cases more than one copy is made. In cases where true "non-stop" operation is needed, rather than some kind of fail-safe or fail-soft back-up, two or more computers may be linked together. Each site will have "two of everything", and the operating system will automatically make a copy of each data change on a separate disk drive. The operating system also monitors, at very frequent intervals, that both processors are functioning and both drives are responding — in the event of a failure, the system first transfers to the non-failed unit and then sets off alarms. In large networks, the second processor or drive on a site may actually be backing up the activity of a different site, and the back-up of the local site may be at a third location.

File Security

It is possible for files to be either private to a particular user or be capable of being shared amongst a number of users in a way which can be flexibly controlled. This involves the operating system in providing various safeguards:

— safety from accidental or malicious access by other users

— safety from accidental damage caused by the owner of the files

— privacy, if needed, with access by either the owner of the files or a specified user or group of users

— safety from hardware or software malfunction.

The necessary safeguards can be achieved by methods such as:

— file access being determined by a combination of user name, number and password

— the mode of access allowed being specified by the owner of the file, eg read only, write, append

— allowing the owner of the file to specify which other users may access his files

— regularly carrying out security dumping to magnetic tape.

Logging

It is essential that the operating system keeps a comprehensive log of all the system actions that relate to a particular user's job. If this information is stored in a system file which is made available to the user it will be of considerable assistance to him in locating the causes of program failure.

Accounting

Many operating systems incorporate accounting routines. A file is set up on which information is recorded on the use of the different parts of the system by each job. Such data would include the amount of CPU time used, the number of disk transfers and the number of lines printed. It is possible to devise quite complex costing systems to ensure that users are charged according to system usage. It may be, for example, that since CPU time is normally at a high premium, this will attract a correspondingly high charge. Alternatively, if an installation has only one line printer, a high charge may be levied for that since excessive use by one user could degrade the performance of the whole system. There is an operational overhead associated with such routines (they are programs, taking up CPU, printing and transfer time) and so care must be taken that the potential recovery is in line with the complexity of the routines used and reports produced. Bureaux always use some form of accounting routine, which may include the accounting facility of the operating system (if there is one), to charge their customers, but many large organisations also treat each service function (such as IT) as a cost centre, and expect other cost centres to pay for their use of the service. Where such a system is used, care needs to be taken that systems are developed to give the required user service and optimum computer use, rather than to produce minimum costs to the user concerned, if there is a conflict between these.

Scheduling

In order to optimise the use of the computer configuration it is necessary to allocate the facilities to the programs according to certain priorities. There are two stages to this.

The first stage is the scheduling of the programs onto the computer according to the priorities imposed by the system and by the users. This is either predetermined by systems staff or allocated by the operations department.

The second stage is the allocation of IAS and peripheral devices and the sequencing of programs within the computer in a multiprogramming environment. This is a function of the scheduling software of the operating system.

To achieve an optimum solution, the scheduling software exclusively controls the allocation and re-allocation of the computer's resources between a number of programs. The aim is, as far as possible, to provide the maximum overlap between CPU time, file accesses and input/output operations.

Under the control of many operating systems, programs are allocated specific areas of storage. Once a program run has been completed, the remaining programs will be repositioned in storage and a new program or programs added to take up the available space. To allow complete flexibility in the choice of programs to be run together, and in the sequence in which they are loaded, every program is written with its own logical numbering of peripheral units and storage locations, rather than the physical identities. In other words, each program is written and treated as an individual job, without reference to other programs which may be present when it is run on the computer. Usually each program is headed with command language statements which indicate its storage and peripheral requirements. When the program is loaded into the machine, the operating system checks to see if sufficient resources are available. If so they are "allocated" to the program which means that the relationship is then fixed between the "logical numbering" used within the program and the actual peripheral numbering and storage locations.

In a "virtual storage" system, programs are written in small units (pages) and one or several pages of a program may be resident in the IAS at any time. Pages are brought in from backing storage as they are required, so the address allocation does not happen until the page is actually loaded. This optimises the use of the computer system, but again it must be noted that there is an overhead involved in page transfer.

The operating system will start programs in the order of assigned priority — usually as a result of the operator supplying a prioritised list of work. When the processing sequence has been determined, the operating system will then notify the operator of any special requirements such as tapes, disc packs, special stationery. This will enable the operator to prepare in advance the items needed for loading, and once again improve system efficiency.

In addition to all this, there is often a facility to inspect the queue and the programs currently being executed, and to change the priority of a program "in flight".

Even the most comprehensive scheduling program is dependent on the skill of the operator in pre-scheduling the jobs entering the system. Only if a reasonable mix of programs is loaded can the scheduler attempt to optimise performance. If, for example, a mix of jobs is loaded which all require the same single peripheral, or which each require a high percentage of the available resources, the task of the scheduler becomes impossible.

Communication with the operator

Communication with the operator is reduced to an absolute minimum. This reduces the chance of operator error and provides, as far as possible, an automatic system. Nevertheless communication is still necessary, either to notify the operator of the current status of programs, or to specify some particular operator action.

The operator communicates with the system (as in individual programs) by way of the console keyboard, in a language which, like the command language, is peculiar to the particular operating system. Messages to the operator would indicate such things as:

— assignment of peripheral units to files

— opening and closing of files

— request to mount or dismount storage units

— notification of error conditions

— request for operator intervention

— start and end of job indications.

Multi-access

A multi-access system is one in which many users can have simultaneous access to a single computer via terminals located either "in-house" or at remote sites. This type of system requires the operating system to share the available resources among a number of users in such a way that each has apparently sole access to the computer. In this situation the computer is obviously multiprogramming. The program is, however, more complicated than in normal batch processing because even though there may be room for, say, three or four typical programs in main store at once, there could be several dozen users "on-line" simultaneously, each using a different program. This means that programs are being shuttled in and out of store very rapidly and require to be held on a fast backing store. With the existence of many independent users, the need for a comprehensive protection and security system is even more crucial than with ordinary multiprogramming.

Originally, operating systems were provided for specific computer systems by the manufacturers with some manufacturers producing a variety of systems to suit their range of CPU sizes and peripheral configurations. This obviously limited the migration of users from one machine to another so manufacturers developed common operating systems across their range of machines.

The next development was manufacturer-independent operating systems. The MicroSoft operating system (MS-DOS) is an example of this for micros and UNIX for larger machines. These are discussed briefly later in this chapter.

4.3 TELEPROCESSING MONITORS

Teleprocessing monitors are software packages which have been developed to handle jobs such as:

— transaction processing, eg stock enquiries, production enquiries, the posting of a cash receipt, order processing

— the transfer of jobs created or generated via processed transactions to a queue of jobs awaiting batch processing

— on-line application program development

— simplification of the tasks of the applications programmer and the systems designer, by providing a set of ready-made facilities.

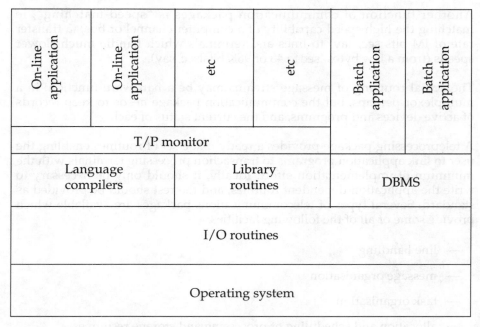

Figure 4.1 Schematic of mainframe software

Teleprocessing monitors in an on-line system must align with the user requirements which govern its implementation. For example, they must provide:

— an acceptable service on a human timescale

— means of recovery from errors

— an interface to other software systems where required, such as operating systems (eg the transfer of jobs to a batch stream) or database management systems.

The teleprocessing monitors effectively form a link between requests for service and the application programs which service such requests and which interface to language compilers, library routines and ultimately to the operating system and hardware. The relationships of the various software entities which surround a teleprocessing monitor are shown in Figure 4.1.

The functional environments of teleprocessing and batch systems differ considerably. The timing of batch system activities is essentially determined within the system, whereas teleprocessing systems must respond to external events within a timescale determined by user requirements.

In effect, a communications package acts as a sub-operating system, which organises the activities within a portion or "partition" of a mainframe computer and, in some cases, an additional "front-end processor" which could be a micro- or minicomputer. In this way the communication tasks are handled separately from the processing, with maximum efficiency.

Another function of communication packages is "speed-matching", ie matching the high speed capability of a computer channel or bus, (a transfer rate of lM bits sec, say) to lines and terminals which handle much slower speeds (from a few bytes/sec to 48 or 96K bitslsec, say).

The actual routeing of message streams may be a hardware function, in a multiplexor perhaps, but the communication package needs to keep records of active devices and programs, and the current status of each.

A teleprocessing package provides a ready made set of routines enabling the user to link application programs to transaction processing terminals with the minimum of implementation effort. Ideally, it should only be necessary to write the application-dependent routines, and the rest should be provided as standard. Several types of telecommunications packages are available which provide some or all of the following facilities:

— line handling

— message organisation

— task organisation

— allocation and scheduling of processing and storage resources

— recovery.

Note that dependent on the actual communication link or network, there may be much more message handling activity on the way between the computer and the terminals, but this will be completely transparent to the system.

Packages are used to speed up implementation. This is true in this area, as in all others. A ready-made and fully tested and proven package, ideally involving no development effort, will be implemented far more quickly than a specially written communication handling routine.

It is important to choose the right package, with the needed facilities. The external interfaces are especially significant. A teleprocessing package or 'monitor' interfaces to users of an on-line system, and optionally to a number of items which may not be part of the monitor itself, such as:

— recovery aids under the control of the operating systems rather than the monitor

— a separate but complementary database management system with which inter-working must occur

— special compilers.

Where several different applications use similar files of data, systems have been developed which allow all the data to be kept in one large linked set of files, which the different applications can use. The maintenance of the linkages and indexes in a large database is a complex operation, usually carried out by a piece of proprietary software called a database management system (DBMS).

Such software will have been produced by computer manufacturers for use in their own machines and by independent companies for use over a range of machines. The facilities of such DBMS software are dealt with in Chapter 7.

4.4 SOFTWARE UTILITIES

These are programs or routines which carry out certain procedures which are common to virtually all applications and installations. They are usually provided by the manufacturer and written in a generalised way so that they may be used in particular cases by means of parameters.

The distinction between utility software and applications packages, which are considered in the next chapter, is that the latter are usually complete systems for specific computer applications, such as payroll, sales ledger, stock control or library management. Utility software is used by most installations for activities common to all, and includes:

— sorting and merging

— housekeeping

— file maintenance

— security

— file copy.

Sorting and merging

Probably the most common utilities wherever serial media (eg tapes) are used are those provided for sorting data. In sequential batch processing, up to 40% of the computer time is spent on sorting, since most applications require data to be presented in a specific sequence. Sorting is the process of arranging records in the desired sequence. The sort process operates on a specific key item or items in a record, and may provide an ascending or descending sequence.

To illustrate this, there may be a requirement to process a number of outstanding invoices in date order; this can be achieved by using the date as the key item. If all the invoices for a particular day are to be presented in value sequence, then the invoice value is a second or minor key. This could beexpressed as sorting by "invoice value within date". Note that the date will probably be in ascending sequence, earliest first, and the value in descending sequence, largest first.

Sort routines are usually provided ready to be tailored by the user to meet particular requirements by specifying a series of parameters. These will specify the layout of the data (record and perhaps block sizes) to be sorted, the size and position of the key or keys, whether ascending or descending sequence is required, and other details such as the type of sort/merge and the name and location of the sorted output. This following list illustrates the features commonly available and illustrates the versatility of sort utilities:

— records can vary in length and format

— keys can be in any fixed position in the record and can be compound, eg Grade/Department/Clock for a sort into Clock number within Department within Grade — Grade being the "major" key, Clock the "minor"

— "own coding" can be inserted at the beginning of the sort routine so that the programmer can carry out selection, editing or similar functions, all as part of the routine

— restart facilities may allow the sort to be restarted at certain points in the data (where there may be several batches to be sorted, available at different times) or during the sort process

— number of peripheral devices or files available, and amount of storage available for the sort.

Some manufacturers supply more than one sort program, appropriate in terms of speed to the different types of file to be sorted. Often a sort program will be in the form of a "generator". The user parameters cause a specifically tailored, non-generalised, program to be produced and in the same way as a program, compiled. This generated program is then stored and used as part of the job-stream, without the need to resubmit parameters every time the sort is run.

If the volume of data is small, the sequence can be obtained very quickly with an IAS sort, ie the data can be sequenced entirely within internal storage.

More often, all the data will not fit into the available IAS, and backing storage has also to be used. There are many sorting techniques, depending on the number and type of peripherals available. Commonly, a sort has several phases. Phase 1 is to read the maximum amount of data into store, sort that and output it to a file. Then the next batch of data is read in, sorted, and added to the original (or a second) file. This continues until all the data is in sorted batches. The next phase is to read two batches, and merge them together in sequence, producing a double-length batch, which is again filed. This phase is repeated until there are just two batches. The final phase is to merge those two onto the desired output file. Since the size of the batch doubles at each pass, it never takes very many passes to complete the sort.

The programmer needs only to know the parameters required for the standard sort/merge software supplied by the manufacturer, and these will be quoted in detail, often with examples, in the appropriate reference manual. In some cases it is possible simply to provide the command SORT (perhaps with parameters) in the source program, and the compiler will provide the necessary routine. There is certainly little need today for programmers to write their own sort programs.

Housekeeping software

There are several processes which every installation has to carry out at some time or another. They include the conversion of data from one medium to another. For example:

— printing of files held on backing store

— printing the contents of the IAS (dumping)

— copying files between different disks or tapes or from one to the other

— backing up (security copying) a fixed disk onto tape, tape streamer, etc.

These functions are all available as utility programs. In some cases, particularly in multiprogramming environments, it may be appropriate to put a job to print out to a backing storage device until the printer is available. It can then be printed either as soon as the printer is free, or later on demand. Different manufacturers use different names for these operations — ICL say "pseudo off-line" printing. "Spooling" was an IBM term, now in common use. (Spool — Simultaneous Peripheral Operation On-Line.) Whatever it is called, it offers more flexibility of use of the computer system, and is particularly valuable in multiprogramming and in network operations (where many users may share one or two printers).

Certain file maintenance procedures, particularly the checking of disk files for excessive use of overflow areas and damaged tracks, and the tidying-up of the files on such media are also common housekeeping tasks.
At the lower end of the scale, it becomes difficult to distinguish between a macro and a utility routine, for example:

— reading and writing of tracks, blocks and sectors

— blocking and unblocking of individual records before or after processing

— file label checking

— floating point arithmetic

— mathematical functions such as square root, tan, sine etc.

Utilities for all these and more are provided by most manufacturers, either as part of the operating system or separately, and should be used by programmers wherever they are appropriate.

4.5 MICROCOMPUTER OPERATING SYSTEMS

Today, the probability is very high that anyone working with data, whether as a programmer, a user manager, a secretary, a typist or any other user, will have a terminal or microcomputer on his or her desk, or will have access to one. Terminals connected to a large machine will have to use the facilities provided on that machine, through the operating system and perhaps a teleprocessing monitor. "Intelligent" terminals, or networked or free-standing microcomputers will have a different set of operating system constraints, even if they have access to data on the main computer.

Before we look at the attributes of operating systems which are specific to microcomputers, it is useful to summarise the general characteristics of operating systems.

They act as the interface between the user and the hardware, facilitating creation and execution of programs. An operating system's main function is to manage access to processor time, internal memory (IAS) and input and output devices. A variety of types of operating systems exist, which may be classified as single- or multi-user. Single-user systems obviously only allow one program to access the facilities, so all are available. In a multi-user system, sharing resources may be necessary, with the operating system determining how they are to be shared, and controlling their use.

Operating systems also differ in the number of programs or processes they allow to run at the same time. Some allow only one, others allow "foreground" and "background" processing (two programs) and yet others allow full multi-programming with many programs appearing to be active at the same time.

Another slightly different classification is the number of tasks which they allow a single process to control at the same time. A multi-tasking operating system allows, for example, file access, processing and printing to operate simultaneously.

For microcomputer operating systems, it is useful to divide the operating environment into three:

— program development

— target-system generation

— run-time.

In large operating systems, there is often no difference between the three, because the system may be developed, tested and then run on the same set of hardware, under the same operating system. However, microcomputer program development may be on a machine suited to that purpose, and there may then be a need to test on a machine similar to the eventual user's machine (the target machine), before finally installing it on that machine for routine running.

A typical program development system will provide the following functions:

— file control

— text editor

— compilers, interpreters, assemblers

— linkers, loaders

— multi-user facilities.

For target-system generation, either the development system will be fully target-machine compatible or final testing will have to take place on a target machine. This could have exactly and only the facilities which the user has, and so any redevelopment would have to be returned to the development system, and then retested.

Run-time facilities on the target machine will typically include:

— run-time control

— memory management

— device management

— file management.

The uses to which these facilities can be put depends on the nature of the application. Some target machines will be general purpose, others dedicated to the application, ie:

— a general-purpose computer employing standard peripherals and used to support a variety of applications

— a dedicated system developed for a special purpose such as a controller embedded in a washing machine or a machine tool.

Here, only the first, the general-purpose computer, is considered. The user is normally concerned with minimising the cost and duration of software development, and will use as much standard system and application software as is relevant. This type of microcomputer application follows conventional industry trends, and there are two broad categories:

— personal micros which are very cheap, sold with minimal if any support, and intended mainly for hobby use, principally with low-cost purchased software, but with a limited program development capability

— micros with commercial-type facilities which offer an alternative to the traditional large and expensive computer.

The low-cost personal micros often have their own dedicated operating system, and offer minimal compatibility between systems. They may use disks for backing storage, but more often have only a cassette interface.

The advent of the IBM PC (Personal Computer) revolutionised the micro market. In this machine, commercial computing on the desk became within the reach of a huge range of people. Other manufacturers — and IBM — developed cheaper, faster, more powerful versions of the PC, most offering compatibility with the IBM PC. This development continues with ever faster processors and clock speeds, more memory and more commercial software.

One of the effects was the sudden demand for standard operating systems which could control machines of different capabilities and from different suppliers. Two such systems are discussed in this chapter, DOS (MS-DOS and PC-DOS) from Microsoft and UNIX from AT&T. All have certain minimal fundamental requirements, foremost amongst which is the ability to handle disks — initially 'floppy disks' (an IBM term) of different sizes and capacities. The floppy disk was initially produced as an alternative to the punched card as a means of capturing data input, but has been developed into a full backing storage medium.

The two basic requirements of a disk Operating System (DOS) are the abilities to handle:

— the physical device

— logical file structures.

The basic DOS has to translate data read or write requests into control signals to select track, wait for sector start, and check for any errors in positioning of the heads or reading/writing the data.

In addition to disk handling, other devices need to be managed, and this includes such requirements as:

— character-by-character device handlers for controlling input and output from keyboards, VDU screens, printers etc

— communication interface handlers, from simple serial asynchronous lines to sophisticated high speed lines

— special device handlers for "non-standard" devices such as graph plotters, scanners, digitisers.

File management software allocates disk storage space for data, and because a data file is commonly fragmented into sectors on different parts of the disk, the software needs to be able to "re-construct" the logical file when it is being read into a program. This implies a need to separate the logical from the physical characteristics of a file, and maintain the links between symbolic file name and physical location(s).

Microsoft DOS

When IBM picked the Microsoft operating system for their PC, the immediate future of DOS was secure. However, there are problems. Naturally, the version of DOS (called PC-DOS) used was tailored to the IBM requirement, and was not identical to other DOS versions. There are now three basic forms of DOS, each one basically the same, but with incompatibilities which can cause difficulties.

The most common form (apart from PC-DOS) is MSDOS — the version found on most competitive products to the IBM PC and its successors.

Some common MSDOS commands include:

— COPY copies a file from a source to a destination

— DIR displays the contents of a directory or sub-directory

— EDLIN allows access to the line editor

— RENAME allows a file to be renamed

— TYPE displays the contents of a file

— DEL removes a file from the directory and makes the space available for re-use.

A feature of MSDOS is a built-in batch processing system using ".BAT" files, including an automatic loader (AUTOEXEC.BAT). Another useful feature is that if a floppy disk is removed and replaced, the new one is automatically accepted by MSDOS. There is a full tree structure for directories n MSDOS, allowing files to be grouped in convenient ways.

A major element available under MSDOS is MS Windows. This allows the user to bring into a panel of the screen part of what would be seen if a program other than the currently displayed one was running on the screen. When several different programs are active, this can be a very important attribute.

UNIX

UNIX was developed from the beginning to be a multi-user, multi-tasking operating system which would be "all things to all people". It is massive, requires not only a large IAS, but also large disk storage to hold it.

As might be expected, the more features that there are, the more complex is the interface with the user. For this reason 'shells' have been produced which effectively translate comprehensible user commands into the detailed requirements of UNIX.

As with DOS, different manufacturers have implemented parts of UNIX which are suited to their particular market and machine, and this has led to a proliferation of versions. However, much of the early confusion which this caused is being resolved as defined sub-sets of UNIX are emerging, allowing UNIX to become a truly general purpose operating system. It can now be implemented on a stand-alone micro (albeit a fairly large one), but is more often found on larger systems, minicomputers and "super-micros", with a Megabyte of memory and 200M bytes or more of hard disk storage.

There are other good operating systems about, but none as widely used as the MSDOS and UNIX systems which we used as examples. There is OS/2, a large operating system like UNIX, but less daunting to the user. Another operating system which is gaining popularity is PICK, with unique facilities which make it the best choice for some configurations and applications.

4.6   CONCLUSION

Operating systems play a crucial role in computers today. They provide an interface with the various input, output and backing storage devices available, thus relieving the programmer of a considerable amount of detailed programming.

These, along with the wide range of utility software available, provide a firm base on which applications can be developed.

On mainframe and minicomputers, each manufacturer has his own operating system. However, on micros there are two major operating systems DOS and UNIX which are widely available on a number of machines. The advantages of using a standard operating system are that it provides a proven environment and facilitates transfer between machines.

NOW TRY THESE . . .

1. List the eight main tasks of a mainframe's operating sohware and write a paragraph on each.

2. Discuss which of the eight main tasks of a mainframe's operating software don't apply in the case of a micro.

3. Distinguish with care between multiprogramming, multi-access, and multiprocessing. Sketch the hardware layout of each style of working.

4. Show how timesharing differs in multiprogramming and multiuser contexts.

5. In a computer system the central processing unit and peripheral devices are co-ordinated by the operating system. State two functions which an operating system might provide.

5 Other software

OBJECTIVES

When you have worked through this chapter, you should be able to:

— state the task of a program language

— briefly compare, with sample instructions, machine coding, assembly language work, and high level programming

— outline the process of assembly and compilation

— compare some major high level program languages

— outline how interpretation and compilation differ

— briefly describe some program development and testing aids

— compare report generators and applications program generators

— list some uses of expert systems

— outline the features of standard applications software

INTRODUCTION

With the advent of general purpose computers has come the need to program them — that is, to provide them with a set of instructions whose execution will cause the computer to produce the required output from a given set of inputs.

Both the programmer and the end user now have a wide variety of tools available to help in the programming process. This chapter looks at the major developments in this area under the following headings:

— programming languages

— microcomputer languages

— program development aids

— testing aids

— report generators

— application program generators

— application packages.

5.1 PROGRAMMING LANGUAGES

This section describes the various levels of programming languages and takes a detailed look at some specific examples.

The lowest level language, "machine code", is made up of the actual instructions, represented in binary, which the machine uses.

The next level is assembly language, in which the programmer uses some form of name or label to refer to specific storage locations, and in which the instructions are represented by symbolic names. Finally, there are the high-level languages in which the programmer writes in a narrative form, which is easier to understand.

This narrative form uses a restricted set of words to which very specific meanings are assigned.

Instructions in a language other than machine code need to be translated into machine code before the computer can use them. Assemblers, compilers and interpreters are the computer programs which do this translation.

Function	Operand Address	Meaning
00100	0000000111	Store the number in store position 0000000111 in the accumulator
00101	0000001000	Add the number in0000001000 to the quantity in the acumulator
10000	0000001001	Move the quantity in the accumulator to store position 0000001001

Figure 5.1   Machine code

Machine code

Machine coding is a one-for-one language. The programmer must write an instruction for every instruction step the machine has to perform to complete a given task. It is found that writing programs at this level results in a great many simple instructions. The process is very time consuming, difficult and vulnerable to mistakes.

Assembly languages

In order to overcome some of the difficulties in programming in machine language, it is possible to write programs using codes for instructions and labels to reference storage locations, provided the computer has the means totranslate them into machine language. This type of program language is called *assembly* and the program to translate it into machine code is called an *assembler*. There is generally a one-to-one relationship between each assembly language instruction and a machine code instruction.

Figure 5.2 shows an assembly language version of the machine code shown in Figure 5.1.

Function	Operand Address	Meaning
L	R1,A	Load the value stored at location A into register 1
A	R1,B	Add the value stored at location B to the value in register 1
ST	R1,C	Store the value in register 1 at location C

Figure 5.2 Assembly language

Assembly languages have been extended to provide *macros*. A macro is a statement within a program which generates more than one machine instruction. They are used where a common sequence of instructions is required, eg in reading or writing data from or to files.

The assembly process

The program written in the assembly language is called the *source program*.

When it is converted or translated into a machine language program it is called the *object program*.

The programmer writes out his instructions on coding forms specially prepared for the job or directly into the machine through a VDU. These instructions are input to the computer, together with the assembler program. The source program is read and translated into machine language by the assembler. The object program which results is (if error-free) ready for the processing of data. It is normal for this object program to be output on some suitable medium such as tape or disk so that it is available for future use without the need for translating or assembling each time. Figure 5.3 illustrates the process.

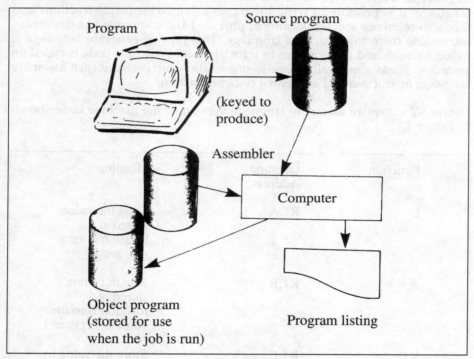

Program

Source program

(keyed to produce)

Assembler

Computer

Object program
(stored for use
when the job is run)

Program listing

Figure 5.3   Assembly process

As well as producing the object program, a list of all the instructions in the program is also produced as an aid to the programmer. This can either be printed or held on disk for access through a VDU. Part of the work of the assembler is to check the coding produced by the programmer for compliance with rules of format and syntax. When errors of this type are detected, diagnostic messages of these errors are displayed again on either the VDU or printed listing for the programmer's attention.

Disadvantages
An assembly language is a low-level language, ie it is nearer to machine code than to everyday English. Being machine-oriented, it requires the programmer to have a good knowledge of the machine. Transfer of assembly

language programs to a machine of a different type is often difficult and, in many cases, impossible.

Programmers who have learnt one assembly language have to learn a different language for a different machine. However, assembly languages are still used because of their efficient employment of machine resources.

High-level languages

As mentioned earlier, there are a number of high-level languages, such as COBOL, FORTRAN, ALGOL, PL/l, Pascal and Ada.

Features

These languages are high-level because the individual instructions are more powerful than the instructions in lower level languages.

The instructions in Figure 5.4 are two high-level language versions of the instructions shown in Figures 5.1 and 5.2.

COBOL

Add A to B giving C

FORTRAN
or
BASIC

C = A + B

Figure 5.4 High-level language

Much more complex formulae may be expressed by using a single instruction in these high-level languages.

In the same way as programs written in assembly language, high-level language programs have to be translated into machine language before processing can be carried out. The principles are similar to those for the conversion of assembly languages. The translation program used is called a compiler, which carries out similar tasks to an assembler. The end-products are an object program, usually on tape or disk, and a compilation listing, normally consisting of the source program statements and an indication of syntax or language errors made by the programmer.

Choosing a programming language

The choice of programming language depends on the availability of an appropriate compiler. If there is an overriding need to use a particular language, the choice of a computer will depend on the availability of a suitable compiler. If a particular computer is installed, language choice is then limited to the compilers which can be obtained for that machine.

The first decision to be made is whether to use a high- or low-level language. For writing applications programs, there is no doubt that a high-level language is preferable. A great deal of systems software can also be written in high-level languages.

A high-level language program is quicker to write and easier to modify. Low-level languages are tailored to specific processor structures and cannot run on other systems.

A decision about which high-level language to use will depend on the nature of the application, the background of the programmer and the reasons for developing the software. BASIC, for example, is very easy to learn and is used quite widely.

Other languages, like Pascal or COBOL, are suitable for programs which will be used commercially and have to be moved around between machines or updated and enhanced regularly.

In order to ensure that programs can be moved between machines it is necessary to have standards. The American National Standards Institute (ANSI) has helped to establish international standards for a number of languages. However, many compilers implement a dialect of the standard with a few extensions or alterations; this lessens the benefits of having a standard in the first place.

Since the development of the "C" language, which has some of the features of both high- and low-level languages, and is widely available on a range of different computer systems, much systems software, and even some application software, particularly for the micro, is written in "C". This ensures portability without sacrificing the run-time speed advantages of assembly language.

Programmers often feel most at home with the first language they learnt, or the language they have worked with most in the recent past. It may be a more effective use of the programmers' time, in some circumstances, for this language to be used rather than another which is in principle more appropriate.

As will be seen in later sections, some software tools such as database management systems may have the facilities within them to create complete applications. However, the following paragraphs describe briefly some of the traditional programming languages in wide use.

The ALGOL family

ALGOL-60 is structured to promote the efficient use of procedures. A large program can be broken up into smaller blocks or procedures. Storage space is allocated dynamically at the time the block is entered and discarded when the block is left. The names used for data items are effective only within the block in which they are specified (declared). Outside the block, the name disappears with the storage space. This makes it possible for particular procedures or modules to be developed, written and tested and then put together within an overall structure. ALGOL-60 is therefore ideal for use with the good programming practices associated with structured programming.

An important decision method in ALGOL-60 is the IF...THEN...ELSE structure. This is a more powerful and elegant form of the BASIC IF...THEN statement because it enables the ELSE option to be specified if the initial condition is not true. IF...THEN...ELSE enables programs to be written with a minimum number of GOTOs, which is one of the criteria used in structured programming. Repetition in ALGOL-60 is implemented with a FOR...DO loop.

ALGOL ideas later produced a whole family of block-structured languages. One of the most significant languages fathered by ALGOL-60 was developed in the early 1970s by Professor Niklaus Wirth of the Zurich Institute of Technology. He named it Pascal after Blaise Pascal, the 17th century French mathematician. Wirth developed it initially as an educational aid to teach computer science.

```
        program addup (input, output);
        var maximum, sum, number, i:integer;
        begin
                sum:=0;
                read(maximum);
                for i:=1 to maximum do
                        begin
                                read(number);
                                sum:=sum+number;
                        end;
                writeln ('Total=' sum);
        end.
```

Figure 5.5 A Pascal program

Figure 5.5 illustrates a Pascal program which adds together numbers typed in at the keyboard and writes the total out to the screen. The indentation aids understanding, particularly of more complex programs than the one illustrated, and is used for structured programming.

Another important language in the ALGOL family is Ada, which was named after another computing pioneer, Lady Ada Lovelace, Charles Babbage's assistant in the nineteenth century. In 1975, the United States Department of

— the Environment Division, which defines the details of the computer resources used

— the Data Division, which defines the files to be used, their formats and any other data area needed

— the Procedure Division, which contains the main body of the program's routines.

The Data Division is particularly important to COBOL. The program procedures in a COBOL program may be less complex than in a scientific algorithm but the file structures are more complex. The full description of a file and its records can be made in the Data Division. Verbs used as instructions in the Procedure Division include MOVE as well as arithmetic and conditional expressions like ADD or GREATER THAN. The latest COBOL standard (COBOL 85) supports good structured programming techniques.

FORTRAN

FORTRAN (FORmula TRANslation) was designed for scientific applications.

ANSI has produced a number of agreed standards for FORTRAN over the years. Compared to later languages, FORTRAN has a primitive structure and set of commands. Decisions, for example, are made by an IF or IF... GOTO statement. FORTRAN was the first scientific high-level language to emerge. There is therefore a great deal of FORTRAN expertise and software, which means that its use continues despite its inadequacies.

PL/1

Another language developed by IBM is PL/1. PL/1 is a high-level language designed to meet the requirements of both scientific and commercial programmers.

Businesses have developed with both IT and scientific programming requirements. To meet these, at least two languages, typically COBOL and FORTRAN, have had to be supported. Further, as management have made more use of computer-aided design and management science, mixed IT and scientific applications have been developed.

Therefore, the need arose for a language containing both scientific and business facilities. It could then be used by scientists and engineers for purely scientific purposes, by IT programmers for business systems and by mixed discipline teams for management science or computer-aided design applications.

The advantage to the IT installation is that it only has to support one high-level language for all purposes and the training programme is simplified. When IBM introduced the System 360, they also announced PL/1, which contains a mixture of COBOL file handling and input/output facilities, FORTRAN input/output and computational succinctness, and ALGOL language structure.

Defence decided it needed a single programming language for its future real-time applications. The language would have to produce programs efficient in the use of resources, reliable in operation and simple to correct or enhance. In 1979, after a series of refinements of the specification (known by names like Starman and Tinman), Ada was eventually chosen. This had been designed by a European team led by Jean Ichbiah of Cll-Honeywell-Bull.

Unlike other high level languages, Ada has been designed to implement the principles of control and correctness embodied in Software Engineering. Control is achieved through the use of separately compiled modules and limited access to sensitive code through restricted visibility. Correctness is obtained by the inclusion of strong typing rules which prevent data defined in one way from being used in any other. More innovative features include the control of parallel processing at a high level through tasking and the creation of re-usable code through generic and library packages.

Structurally Ada is similar to Pascal, with the same potential for use in many kinds of applications. Its features make it the most advanced third generation language, especially as it has specifically attempted to address the problems of portability, reliability and maintenance too a much greater degree than others. Ada's main disadvantage is that compared to other languages, the development time is longer, but the integration of Ada with an APSE (Ada Program Support Environment), providing appropriate development tools for the programmer will reduce this.

BASIC

BASIC (Beginner's All-purpose Symbolic Instruction Code) became popular in the late 1970s with the spread of microcomputers, although it had been developed much earlier.

BASIC is excellent for its original purpose, which is to serve as an effective language for beginners and non-computer specialists. There are modern structured versions of BASIC as well as BASIC compilers.

COBOL

When commercial applications started to grow in the late 1950s, it became clear that a standard language was needed for typical business Information Technology (IT) applications. These involve the manipulation of large volumes of information organised in a similar structure to files in a traditional filing cabinet.

In 1961, the first specification was produced for COBOL (COmmon Business Oriented Language).

COBOL programs are divided into four parts called divisions:

— the Identification Division, which contains the program name, and other identifying information

Programming languages summary

COBOL is the most widely used programming language in commercial installations. Because of this, COBOL will continue to be widely used until the procedural type of language is no longer required. This is likely to be when application generators have been available for at least ten years and when the early applications have been rewritten.

In the scientific field FORTRAN and Pascal will continue to be used. PL/1 has not made the impact that might have been expected. This is largely because of the vast investment most companies have in COBOL.

One language, CORAL, a development of ALGOL, has been widely used in real-time systems. However, Ada is now superseding most other real-time languages both for the development of military and civilian command and control systems, (eg air-traffic control), and commercial and financial applications (eg banking).

5.2 MICROCOMPUTER LANGUAGES

Like early mainframe computers, the first micros were programmed in machine language or assembler code. However, this situation did not last for long. BASIC language interpreters and, in some cases, compilers were quickly introduced. BASIC is now to the micro what COBOL is to the mainframe.

Because of the difficulties in using BASIC to handle complex file and data structures, many other languages have been developed. These include versions of most of the mainframe languages, eg COBOL, CORAL, ALGOL and FORTRAN already mentioned. Additional languages include the following:

— APL

— C and C++

— FORTH

— LISP

— LOGO

— PILOT

— PROLOG

These languages are not normally used for major commercial programming activities. However, each is useful in specific areas.

APL was originally developed for mainframe computers and requires large amounts of main memory and backing storage. It is designed to make the input of mathematical calculations and data simpler. Its main use to date has been financial planning. Its main drawback is that it uses a special character set not readily available on smaller machines.

C is a well structured language and it is easy to transfer programs written in C from one machine to another. It is highly suited to systems programming work, in fact, many compilers have been written in C. However, it is not an easy language to learn, read or understand.

PROLOG and *LISP* are a new class of language designed to facilitate the structure of inference programs. They will no doubt come into their own in knowledge-based systems. *LOGO* is a development of *LISP* which has been used to develop Computer Based Training (CBT) packages. *PILOT* is another CBT language but simpler in that it has fewer facilities, ie the programmer has to do more coding to achieve the same objectives.

FORTH has been developed as a real-time language. It is very versatile and can easily be extended by users who have the facility to define new functions. It, too, has been used in the CBT environment.

There are four main ways in which these languages are processed to run on a given machine. They are via:

— an interpreter

— a compiler producing intermediate code which is then run through an interpreter

— compilers

— a cross-compiler.

5.3 INTERPRETERS

Interpreters work by taking a language statement, interpreting it at run time and then performing the action required. Typically, each line of code is given a unique number. If a line has to be changed it need only be retyped. The program can then be run incorporating the modification. The major drawbacks of interpreters are that the speed of execution is slower than a compiled program and that the interpreter and program must always be held in store. No attempt can be made to optimise the running of the program.

In the case of *compilers producing intermediate code*, the program is compiled in the traditional way. However, instead of producing machine code, a machine-independent code is produced which can then be optimised for storage and processing time. For any given machine, all that is required is an interpreter for this code. The code can be very compact and thus the net result is reasonably efficient. Some translators supply an additional stage called "native-code generation" that will compile the intermediate code to the machine code of the target machine. One of the advantages of this system is that by producing intermediate code interpreters for several machines, the same source code program can be run on different systems.

When dedicated systems are being produced and efficiency is of the utmost priority, then a full *compiler* will be needed. Good high-level language compilers can be almost as efficient as the best hand-coding in machine language.

The system for which a program is being written may be very limited in size, and may be too small to be used for software development. In this case, a development system is needed that allows for the programming and testing of software on a larger machine. When development is finished a cross-compiler is used, which compiles programs on the development machine but produces code for smaller machines. This code could take the form of intermediate code for an interpreter or be in the second machine's own machine language.

Another area of development specific to microcomputers is in the use of software which was originally designed to allow end-users to specify, build and then access their own files, but which now offers something close to a structured programming language. Most of the database management systems for micros fall into this category, and the foremost is possibly the Ashton Tate dBase family of products.

A current, well proven product is dBase, and offers the user the opportunity to maintain and extract reports from his or her own files, interactively through the keyboard and screen or printer. It also offers a way of writing and storing sequences of actions, and repeating them on demand — in other words, programming. dBase III is an interpreted language, dBase IV optionally produces intermediate code. Both are slow, as was noted earlier, but there are products such as Clipper from Nantucket Inc which will compile and link dBase language statements (with some alterations) into large but fully compiled machine code which run much more quickly. dBase IV offers all kinds of facilities to both user and programmer, including SQL (Structured Query Language) which enables the specification of a system through the data, rather than through procedures, in much the same way as Jackson Structured Analysis defines a system through the data. Application generators (see later) and similar features are included also.

Another area where the boundary between the programmer and the microcomputer user is less clear is in the application of "spreadsheets". Basically, a spreadsheet is an array of rows and columns of "cells", each of which can contain data, and each of which can be related to others by formulae. The simplest case is where the last column and last row in a table are to hold the arithmetic sum of all previous rows and columns. This is specified to the spreadsheet program before data is entered, and then any data entered anywhere is more or less instantly reflected in the appropriate row and column total. Complex relationships can be specified, and the resulting spreadsheet can act as stock records, financial ledgers, parts explosions, order files and so on.

Both these examples are forms of high-level language programming, and there are very many good and reliable products on the market. The range of traditional languages and less traditional approaches and implementations is substantial.

Whilst the full potential of the microprocessor cannot be achieved without good high-level language implementations, the prospective programmer is faced with the problem of selecting the best method for his purpose.

The importance of using a high-level language and taking a rational approach to the selection of the correct language for a project cannot be over-emphasised.

5.4 PROGRAM DEVELOPMENT AIDS

The need to improve programmer productivity has long been recognised. This has given rise to a whole set of tools to help all the stages from initial system design right through the development and testing stages to implementation. In this and the following sections we will begin by looking at a range of individual tool applications in program development, next at some areas where testing aids can be used, as report generators, and then consider some of the more extensive tools which offer development aid to such an extent that the need for programming work as such is practically eliminated. The individual tool applications which we will cover are:

— program file creation and maintenance

— flowcharters

— decision table preprocessors

— VDU screen formatters.

Many of the software tools referred to will be included in a general operating system. Those that are not can be made available either as bought-in or in-house products, as a lot of programming effort can be saved by their availability and use.

Program file creation and maintenance

Most operating systems include a text editor, which can be used for the creation and maintenance of program files. Since the most obvious method of indicating a required change to source code is to annotate the latest compiler-generated listing, a text editor must include the facility of context searching. In addition, it should enable alterations to text to be simply controlled, ideally by quoting a "before and after" format. When programmers are working in an interactive environment, familiarity with the local text editor is essential. The availability of a context search makes a text editor a suitable tool for use during program testing. Instead of producing vast quantities of printed output, a test run is made which generates an output file, which is then examined by using the editor. Most editors allow a buffer or page of information to be examined in any "direction", and much time can be saved by making sensible use of a context search. This technique is particularly useful when dealing with compilation errors during program development.

Other useful tools for file maintenance include facilities for copying, renaming and deleting files. In an interactive environment, it is particularly important that unwanted files are purged from the system as soon as practicable, whereas safe copies of master files must be readily created.

Flowcharters

The flowcharter takes the source code of the compiled program and from it constructs a computer-produced flowchart. This is particularly useful for comparison with the original flowchart to check that the code, with all modifications, still conforms to the logic of the original specification. The original flowcharts, or the code, can then be amended as necessary.

Decision table preprocessors or interpreters

Both of these can be used to produce object code which is suitable, after testing, for running as production programs. Alternatively, they can be used for checking the validity of logic expressed in decision table form. They provide a means of taking miniature specifications and converting them directly into code.

Screen formatters

The formatting of screens for on-line systems used to be a tedious exercise. Screen formatters have been developed to improve this area. The user can sit at a screen with an analyst and plan out the format for the VDU. When he is satisfied with it, a record of the screen layout can be made which is then subsequently processed to provide the necessary code to support the format. This technique also forms part of many report and application generators.

5.5   TESTING AIDS

A second set of aids has been developed to improve the testing of programs. These include:

— trace and snapshot

— test generators

— test harnesses

— interactive debugging.

Trace and snapshot

A very useful feature of trace software is to monitor the path of a program run and at each statement of the source program print out:

— the statement or the statement line number

— the contents of the main registers

— the contents of the accumulators.

The programmer then has a complete record of a path through his program and the value of the variables as they are retrieved, calculated and stored. This is a very powerful, but slow, software aid and the output obtained is voluminous.

The better trace programs allow the user to switch the trace facility on and off at various points in the program. In some, the trace can be actioned retrospectively. Thus, the trace program will print out the last, say, 32 statements, or routine names, passed prior to the failure point. This is achieved by the software holding a cyclic store of 32 elements, each of which contains either a statement, statement number or routine name. As the program passes down its path, this cyclic store is updated by having the appropriate identifier added and after reaching the total of 32, overwriting the earlier statements. This can be very useful in tracing the path up to a failure without incurring the volume of a full trace.

With snapshot software the user indicates the points at which he wants the program under test to be halted. At these points the snapshot program "dumps" specified stores and then restarts the test program automatically.

Test data generators

Faced with the problem of providing test data, the programmer should consider using the computer to generate specific formats of data. Although in some cases it will be necessary to write a specific test data generator, software is available which will generate test data to most required formats on various media.

The facilities provided by the generator should include:

— a *random number generator* which can produce a variety of distributions within specified limits, and be able to generate appropriate check digits

— an *alpha-numeric string generator* which should produce strings of alpha-numeric characters of a fixed length or variable lengths, eg 7 characters long, or between 1 and 5 characters long and produce strings with one or more characters fixed, eg the last two characters Z0 or the first characters always alphabetic

— a *file generator* which should be able to generate files with fixed or variable length records, generate records with constant fields, eg one field always containing "shop", and another always containing "2001". In addition it should be able to generate records with specified fields, eg a key field, containing a number larger than that on the previous record or sorted on several keys, if required

— an *expression generator* which should generate values for variables as a function of the values of other variables, eg generate a total of a column of variables

— a *variable generator* which should produce variables in which, unless specified differently, the correct type of variable is deduced from the program, eg character, binary, floating point, etc

— a *formatted data generator* which should produce data to a specified format; this will be used mainly for input

— an *explicit data generator* which should list explicit values for data and permutate their order and generate data to test the program particularly at the extremes, eg maximum and minimum values for data

— an *error case generator* which should generate random or specified errors in the data, eg data outside range, or of the wrong type or of an incorrect format and be able to set a limit to the number of errors if random errors are produced.

The above facilities will allow a programmer to generate, by user commands, test data to the various formats required to test his program(s) and in sufficient volume to allow exhaustive testing to take place.

Interactive debugging

The system of testing of most mainframe installations in recent years has been "closed shop" testing. The programmer submits his tests to the operations department, the operators carry them out according to his instructions and return the results to the programmer. The programmer does not even have to enter the computer room, hence, the term "closed shop".

Most of the facilities that have been described in the earlier sections belong to this batch processing "closed shop" environment. However, with the advent of multiprogramming and, in particular, multi-access, using terminals, it is possible to have interactive testing. The multiprogramming operating system ensures that the efficiency of the computer system is not significantly degraded.

On this type of system the use of interactive debugging is growing. Claims of a 20 per cent decrease in the cost of debugging, over that of batch processing testing by submission, have been made. It is not suggested that interactive debugging replaces dry running and desk checking and these must continue to play an important part in reducing test costs. Interactive testing can reduce the total time of testing by giving the programmer better facilities for machine debugging.

Most interactive systems have special incremental compilers. The major facilities of such a system are described below:

— it should communicate with the programmer in the terms of the source language

— it should allow the programmer to stop his program at a pre-arranged instruction or statement

— it should be capable of stopping the program whenever a condition specified by the programmer is satisfied, eg when a counter reaches a certain figure or when a buffer is full

— at any halt, the programmer should be able to access an item of data or part of memory and be able to print their values

— the programmer should be able to insert, delete or alter his source program or any item of data, and then allow the program to restart at any selected point

— the programmer should be able to step his program on one instruction at a time

— trace facilities with the option of switching the trace on or off should be available

— if an unexpected fault occurs, the system should restore control of the test to the programmer at his terminal.

Provided that testing is adequately planned, interactive testing provides an economical and efficient way of debugging programs because the programmer has close contact with his testing.

5.6 REPORT GENERATORS

Programming a computer to carry out a specified task is not easy. Even when the task is well defined and a good design for the system achieved, the translation of that design into a working program requires significant skill and effort.

Programming tools are now evolving which aim to limit the resources needed to convert a user requirement into an efficient program.

Although these tools are collectively known as "program generators", they fall broadly into two categories:

— report generators

— applications program generators.

The production of reports has been a major feature of most commercial computing systems. A report generator is a software utility which has been specifically designed to enable such reports to be programmed easily and rapidly.

The most common form of report generator is effectively a high-level language translator, which accepts as input a "program" written in a highly problem-oriented language and generates a machine language program from it; The input language is easy to learn and, because of the formal and restricted nature of the commands, it is easier to ensure that the logic is correct. Two of these languages are RPG, developed by IBM, and FILETAB from NCC.

Report generators are designed mainly to produce line-printer reports from files stored on a variety of media. In addition, many of the functions expected of a commercial language (such as COBOL) may be performed; for example, maintaining files, performing calculations, looking up tables and branching to library sub-routines in other languages.

The specifications necessary to define the problem and control the generator are often entered directly into the system through VDUs, as a set of parameters.

Parameters will define such things as:

— *file description*, which specifies file names, input and output devices associated with these files

— *input*, which is a description of record layout of input files, identifying the records by name

— *output*, which is a description (or picture) of the layout of records or output files, controlling the timing of their output by means of control breaks

— *calculation*, which specifies the operations on the input data, and on intermediate data produced from other calculations required to produce the output.

By far the best way of describing the contents of a report file is by means of a decision table. FILETAB enables a decision table to be used directly as input, thus reducing the chances of error by further simplifying the procedure.

Report generators provide a concise system, whereby non-technical staff and management can answer simple enquiries involving retrieval and report generation. Using such a generator, IT staff may simply and quickly carry out quite complicated tasks associated with reporting, enquiries, updating and the creation of files. Although a report generator is not as comprehensive as, say, COBOL, it can save considerable programming effort in many data processing applications; one large company recently reported an increase in programming productivity of 80 per cent after changing to FILETAB.

5.7 APPLICATIONS PROGRAM GENERATORS

The term application program generator (APG) covers a wide range of software products which vary from code generators, through systems generators and application generators on to application development systems. If correctly used, these represent various levels of service to the program producer who might not necessarily be a programmer.

Most IT activities consist of:

— data input and validation

— file update

— data output and report production.

The APGs are designed to do some or all of these tasks. They differ from report generators in that most report generators provide a fixed logic, whilst most APGs allow the programmer to provide the logic. In some instances, however, the APG will provide a fixed logic, eg for the sequential update of a master file.

Scope	Method
Input definition	— Screen painting
— Data definition/update	— Form filling
— Procedure definition	— Questionnaire
— Report/Enquiry definition	— Commands

Figure 5.6 Scope and method of application

APGs produce one of two sorts of output, either a program language code such as COBOL which is then compiled and can be run separately from the APG or a code specific to that APG which has to be run in conjunction with the APG which acts as an interpreter.

The difference is important. In the former case the code produced can be modified independently of the APG. In the latter case, however, any modifications have to be done to the original code.

In both cases it may be possible to insert pre-coded or pre-compiled routines.

The APGs can be classified according to their scope and method of application (Lobell, 1983). These classifications are shown in Figure 5.6.

The scope is a variation on the major IT activities listed at the beginning of this section. The method is the approach which an APG uses to produce that component of a program. The figure shows the general relationship between the two. APGs will have these facilities in different degrees.

Input definition

This is concerned with the processing requirement of data input and validation. The major method used is similar to that of screen formatting described in the section on development aids. It is sometimes called prototyping or screen painting. However, it usually goes beyond the simple screen formatting and provides for the linking of a sequence of screens and the generation of all the screen handling code.

Data definition update

APGs are generally associated with Data Dictionaries (DD) and Database Management Systems (DBMS). These may be built into the generator or coversely the generator may be part of or an add-on to such systems. The user of an APG defines his data requirements to the APG by means of form filling. This helps to provide a checklist of requirements and also establish the links with the DBMS. Having done this, both enquiry and update routines can be specified without the user having to worry about file accessing.

Procedure definition

There are a number of possible approaches here:

— pre-defined procedures

— very high-level language

— re-usable blocks of code

— conventional high-level language.

Pre-defined procedures can cover a large number of situations. Report generators are a specific type of pre-defined procedures, as are standard sort and merge programs. In APGs they are normally parameterised and the user can modify them to suit his needs through questionnaires or form filling or even an appropriate command language.

The use of a *very high-level* language provides a second method of defining processing requirements. These languages tend to support the structured approach to programming and are usually easier to use than languages like PL/1, COBOL or BASIC.

Typically 60 to 80 per cent of an application's requirements can be met through the use of *re-usable* blocks of code. These blocks are created as "skeletons" to be "fleshed out", again using form filling or questionnaires.

The use of a *conventional high-level* language provides a mechanism which allows the programmer to code up routines which are beyond the scope of the APG.

Report definition

This process is similar to that used for report generators. It is possible to use any of the four methods to describe to the APG the report format and content.

Enquiry definition

APGs usually have a facility to produce responses to simple enquiries. These can be given through a form filling routine or via a questionnaire. However, a *command language* often provides the most flexible approach. It enables the user to specify his enquiry succinctly and thoroughly but it does have the disadvantage that it has to be specifically learnt.

Application generators summary

Application generators have dramatically increased programmer productivity. Some suppliers claim up to 80 per cent improvement on conventional methods. They also have two other advantages:

— user involvement

— prototyping.

Because of the way in which APGs work, the user can be involved with the programmer in producing screen layouts, report layouts and, to some extent, processing procedures. Through this involvement he is much more committed to the final system.

Prototyping, that is producing a version of a system and trying it out, is also practical because development times are much reduced.

The use of APGs is going to increase rapidly over the next few years, with conventional programming being relegated to the maintenance of existing systems.

Expert systems

A completely different approach to application generation is in the area of "Expert Systems". The concept is that if all the knowledge and methodology of an expert can be filed in a way which allows a system to respond to questions in the same way that the expert would, the system can become the expert. If many experts in a field all supply their knowledge, in theory the system becomes better at answering questions than any single expert.

This can be approached in different ways, one of the most straightforward being the question and answer technique, in which the computer system, when building the database, is told what questions to ask, and what the next question should be depending on the answer received. The computer system effectively "learns" to ask the right questions to enable it to arrive at a point when it can make a definitive statement, as a result of its questioning. An early attempt to produce such an expert system was in the field of medical general practice. A patient could sit, in some waiting-room facility offering privacy, in front of a screen and some (possibly simplified) keyboard or other input device. By answering a range of questions, possibly with multiple choice answers selected by touching the screen or a defined button or key, the patient enables the system to make a preliminary diagnosis which could be supplied to the GP when the consultation takes place.

There are other approaches, all of which enable the system to acquire information, store it with contextual links, and thus retrieve it when appropriate input is made. The acquisition of information and the access to it need not be separate stages. Some systems integrate the two, becoming more and more responsive and accurate as the interaction with the expert proceeds. Ambiguities of language can be resolved immediately, so that the actual dialogue can be very close to natural language.

Expert systems exist in small ways in many places, and there are also large systems which approach the ideal. An illustration of a small "expert system" is a simple word processor which is intended to help occasional users by "guessing" what a word will be from the letters typed so far. The system offers a choice of words in a pop-up list, with the word being typed at the foot, and while building its own dictionary of words it remembers those used most frequently and offers them. If this were typed on such a system, the user would only have to type "sy" for the system to fill the word out to "system" since it is very frequently used. This is more of a "game" than an expert system, but it illustrates the way in which the power of the computer can be used to assist in decision making — which is the purpose of expert systems.

Software tools

It is always seen as a large and potentially costly step to move from traditional "hand-carved" programming, based on manually documented analysis and design work, to one of the major workbenches or a Fourth Generation Language (4GL). Yet the benefits are enormous. An analysis, design and documentation workbench, such as Excelerator based on a micro, provides a systems analyst with all the tools required to produce, modify and verify specifications quickly and accurately. The cost of correcting an error in a specification increases exponentially as the development progresses.

Preventing such errors at the start not only reduces cost but speeds development. A 4GL allows the developer to concentrate on what has to be done, rather than how it is done, by one of a number of approaches. Such approaches include spreadsheets, perhaps associated with database management, relational database handling, application generation, form- filling, procedural languages and simple menu selection. Any of these will produce error free machine code (or intermediate code), and will allow complex interactions between data sets to be simply, quickly and accurately specified.

Applications which once took months to develop can now be completed in days, and are so readily tuned to the users' current requirement that the tools available deserve more use than they get. Any application generator is a form, albeit a very limited form, of expert system, since it provides its existing information to the user for tailoring to the real situation presented, and remembers what has been done.

However—the same principle applies to the selection of a tool as was stated in the selection of a language—it must be done carefully and the right tool must be chosen from the large number available. The NCC, as part of the British Government N Starts N initiative, have produced tool samplers for hands-on testing of a range of products, and have exhaustive information about very many software tools.

5.8 APPLICATION PACKAGES

An applications package can be defined as a program, or set of programs, covering a specific function, eg payroll, designed for use in more than one environment or organisation.

The routine accounting and basic IT applications have been supplied by bureaux, software houses and consultants for many years. More complex applications such as production control, linear programming and project management are also available.

To give some appreciation of the wide potential use of packages, it is worth listing some of the types of packages available:

production control	— production scheduling
	— bills of material processing
	— parts explosion and listing
	— shop loading
	— cost centre performance
	— labour costing
stock control inventory management	— forecasting
	— automatic stock replenishment
	— costing
	— purchase order preparation
payroll	— piece work calculations
	— bonus calculations
	— gross to net calculations
	— tax calculations
	— year end tax accounting
accounting/costing	— sales ledger
	— sales analysis
	— credit control
	— purchase ledger
	— nominal ledger and monthly manage-ment accounts
	— costing
other uses	— share registration
	— mailing lists
	— critical path analysis (PERT)
	— discounted cash flow (DCF)
mathematical	— linear programming
	— vehicle scheduling
	— deposit siting
engineering	— computer aided design (CAD)
	— loading calculations and framework analysis
	— computer aided manufacture (CAM)

The above are just a selection of the variety available and there are many packages in each category.

Using packages

The standard of packages varies; some are completely documented, making it relatively simple for the potential user to evaluate whether they meet his requirements; others have inadequate documentation for evaluation. This lack of documentation makes the modification to commercial packages which is necessary in most organisations, extremely hazardous.

The larger systems packages are generally modular in construction, permitting the user to select the parts relevant to his needs. It is possible to modify a package, but it should be appreciated that modification of a complex package is difficult. It also means, in most cases, that if the supplier subsequently updates the package, the enhanced version will not be usable without a similar user modification.

From the users' point of view a good, flexible, well documented package represents a way for him to benefit from a computer much more quickly and economically on an "off the peg" basis rather than by developing his own tailor-made system. Further, he may be able to use applications and techniques which he could not afford to develop with his own resources.

If the package has been widely used, it will have been tested under a great variety of conditions and therefore should be free from systems or programming errors. Subsequent enhancements, particularly those which are government imposed like tax charges, decimalisation or metrication, are supplied free or at a small additional cost.

In view of these advantages it is disturbing to find from NCC surveys that organisations have in the past been reluctant to use packages. This has been due to four main reasons:

— management's attitudes that "our organisation's problems and systems are, and must be, unique"

— computer personnel's arguments that "packages are inefficient in their use of the computer's capacity"

— lack of support by the package suppliers — notably computer manufacturers — in carrying out a feasibility study in the use of a package and in its implementation

— bad marketing by the suppliers in identifying the user's real needs; in publicising the use of particular packages and in providing inadequate documentation.

These attitudes are changing and the demand from users for good packages is increasing. These are being supplied in ever increasing numbers by the manufacturers, software houses and bureaux. It is expected that packages will account for a high percentage of the anticipated increase in computer usage in the future.

However, users should remember that packages are not a substitute for trained, experienced staff. These need not necessarily be programmers but certainly they need to understand the workings of the package and how it can be adapted by the use of the various parameters.

IBM, in the introduction to one of their packages, state:

This manual only introduces the basic principles of scientific inventory management. For a company to apply these principles properly someone in the company must be completely familiar with every aspect of this powerful new tool.

People are generally either for or against packages. The reasons may be subjective, such as "pride of authorship" or "not made here" attitudes. They may be objective — the package is too early, too late, too sophisticated, not sophisticated enough, incapable of doing what is required.

A good package should be well documented, easy to change (when necessary), economical and easy to use. If any of these four factors is missing, there will be problems during implementation.

To implement a package, all the tasks of implementing any system must be covered — system modification, system testing, user training, file conversion, changeover. As a minimum, the documentation required will be:

— user manual

— operations manual

— system specification.

Advantages and disadvantages
Some benefits of using packages are that they can provide the expertise which may not be available within the organisation and will be costly to acquire. Minimum programming effort is needed, and packages use (or may use) less machine time during testing. Implementation may therefore be speedier. There is a likelihood of fewer design errors if the package is in use in a number of installations; the approach will be standard with common applications. In addition, the package can be evaluated in a user situation.

There are, however, disadvantages. Poorly designed packages can be inflexible and inefficient because of the need to suit a variety of users. They can be difficult to maintain, particularly if they are modified to suit the installation (future modifications and enhancements may no longer fit it).

5.9 CONCLUSION

The programming of computers has come a long way since the days when programs were written in machine code. Most new systems will be written using application development packages which are becoming more sophisticated.

The "user interface" to a traditional programming language is more or less unfriendly, depending on the way text editing and debugging aids are provided. There has been a movement away from the need to use a normal "QUERTY" keyboard to provide short cuts. This is usually described as "WIMPS", for Windows, Icons, Mice and Pointers. Pull-down, pop-up and bar menus allow "multiple choice" selection of a desired feature. Icons are miniature pictures of the thing to be selected. A mouse is a desktop rollerball which is programmed to move a pointer on the screen as the ball is moved, allowing selection of a menu item or an icon. Some aspects of this trend are advantageous, because they avoid the need for memorising "control character strings", but they are expensive in use of memory. However, they do allow users without traditional computer programming or systems skills to use computers effectively, and can also be very helpful to computer people when intelligently incorporated into workbenches and similar development aids.

The best of the development aids will be able to provide screen formatting facilities, a link into a data dictionary and access to files either through conventional techniques or via a database.

The role of the analyst and designer will be geared even more closely to determining the users' needs. The programmer will use the machine to implement these requirements.

The use of application packages is going to increase; this will particularly apply to small businesses. In this situation the task of the analyst is to find a package which meets the users' business requirements.

The need for programmers will not disappear, but their role will change. They will be required to write the packages.

NOW TRY THESE . . .

1. A firm has a large computer system with many interactive VDUs used in offices, factory and warehouse. Discuss, with reasons, the advantages and disadvantages of such a system compared with a manual system.

    (a) State briefly the main difference between a compiler and an interpreter.

    (b) Why is interpretation ohen more suited to small computers than compilation?

2. Discuss this statement — desktop publishing is a superb extension of word processing.

3. Use a spreadsheet for one of the following; record what you did and the problems found:

    (a) your own accounts for a week

    (b) analysis of the results of a survey (eg market research)

    (c) producing multiplication tables

    (d) holding a page of a tutor's mark book

4. Use a business graphics program to display data from the last question (or elsewhere) in different forms. When is it best to use each of line graph, bar chart and pie diagram?

5. In an office, what do people mean by "integrated package"?

6. Use a word processor to prepare brief notes for a beginner on how to use the word processor.

7. Make a table comparing the features of a word processor with those of an electric and an electronic typewriter.

    (a) Explain what word processing is and describe briefly the software facilities a word processing system might provide

    (b) Give an example of one organisation in which the introduction of a word processing system would be of value. Explain what the benefits might be.

8. Some people call the modern IT-based office "the paperless office". Is it possible to work entirely without paper?

6 Systems

OBJECTIVES

When you have worked through this chapter, you should be able to:

— compare the main factors of system design and show how they may balance in practice

— outline the technique of batch processing, with some uses

— outline the technique of on-line working, with some uses

— give examples of real-time systems and list their main features

— explain the nature of distributed processing

— list some advantages of small business systems over using a large computer

— outline major aspects and uses of office automation and compare with traditional methods of working

— briefly describe some approaches to office automation.

INTRODUCTION

At an early stage in defining a new system, the systems analyst must have a clear understanding of the objectives of the design which must be established by management.

These initial objectives will almost certainly be modified during the early stages of systems analysis as the detailed system requirements became more apparent. It is important that the design objectives should be formally agreed before any choice of systems options is made.

6.1 DESIGN ASPECTS

There is usually more than one way of achieving a desired set of results although some methods may have their drawbacks.

The acceptable design is likely to be a compromise between a number of factors, including cost, reliability, accuracy, security, control, integration, expansibility, and acceptability.

Cost

Cost is associated with the two activities of development and operation. Development comprises all the stages from the initial investigation to the successful handover of a live system to the users. Operation also includes maintenance of the system. It is very rare for any computer-based system to run for years without substantial changes being needed to allow for changing business requirements or improvements in hardware and software. In fact, it is the experience of many long-established computer installations that the major part of their analysis and programming effort is devoted to maintaining existing systems. Clearly an important objective is to minimise costs in these areas.

Reliability

This includes the robustness of the design, availability of alternative computing facilities in the event of breakdown, and the provision of sufficient equipment and staff to handle peak loads (whether seasonal or cyclical).

Accuracy

The level of accuracy needs to be appropriate to the purpose. For instance, the accounts of an individual customer will probably be kept to the nearest penny, whereas the monthly sales total for a region may only be required to the nearest £1,000. For each defined level a balance needs to be achieved between avoidance of error and the cost of avoiding the errors.

Security

There are many aspects of security, but those which particularly concern us are confidentiality, privacy, and security of data.

Confidentiality of certain information is vital to the success of a firm. It could cause severe damage if it fell into the hands of competitors. The system has to ensure that only authorised staff have access to such information.

Privacy concerns information about the individual employee or members of the employee's family. If the personnel file or the payroll file is held on the computer, the design of the system must guard against any unauthorised access to this information.

Data security (often called "data integrity") is also significant. If the data held on computer files is incorrect, then the system objectives cannot be achieved. Measures are needed to guard against alteration or destruction of data, whether accidental or intentional.

Control

The system should give management the facility to exercise effective control over the activities of the organisation. One aspect of this control is the provision of relevant and timely information. This provision is made much more useful by the ability to extract important information from the mass of available but less important information; this is the principle of 'exception reporting'. Also important is the ability to produce ad hoc reports. Another essential feature is routine control of goods and monies handled to include balancing routines which automatically highlight problems.

Integration

Before the advent of a computer, it was usual for each department to keep its own records. This means that it was possible to keep multiple sets of records on the same basic data. The reconciliation of these sets of data, one with another, caused major problems. These resulted from errors in transcription, from source documents being mislaid, or simply from the time-lag between an action occurring (for instance, an item being withdrawn from stock) and the occurrence being entered on the various sets of records.

In addition, each set of records was only easily accessible to the department which raised the set, and generally only to one person at a time.

Ideally, when a computer-based system is being designed, all files relating to a given item of information should be automatically updated as a result of a single input. However when this is achieved, the control of the input documents becomes even more important. We must be concerned, therefore, not simply with the computer procedures, but also with the clerical procedures in user departments and/or the computer operations department.

A further danger is that different systems which make use of any item of information may be designed at different times. Consistent documentation is vital to ensure control is maintained.

Expansibility

Any system needs to be able to cope with seasonal or cyclical variations in volume. Estimates need to be made of volume trends for the expected life of the system. If there is any doubt about the capacity of hardware or software to handle future volumes, a clear upgrade path, particularly for hardware, must be identified.

Acceptability

Even a system which the designer believes to be perfect will fail unless it has the support of the user departments and management, as well as the programming and operations staff.

A system which affects people (and there are very few systems which do not) needs to be agreed by staff representatives, possibly the relevant trade unions, as well as by the individuals whose jobs will be changed. An unconvinced or disgruntled user is quite capable of sabotaging the most elegant system (consciously or unconsciously) if only by exaggerating any "teething troubles" which occur during implementation.

Approval for a system may be required from people outside the company. A really big customer may lay down rules for invoice presentation which management may be unwilling to dispute.

The company's auditors will also need to approve any parts of the system which impinge on assets or accounts.

6.2 THE AVAILABLE OPTIONS

Costs, response time and pay-off

Many of the considerations which will be discussed in this chapter are dictated by the response time, and/or turnaround time, which the user requires and obtains from a computer system.

Response time is the time taken by a system to respond to a given input. This will vary according to the type of application and must be optimised to meet the user's demands. Systems in the real-time category may respond in seconds or minutes; other on-line systems may take an hour or so before a transaction is processed. In a chemical plant response time may be the interval between reading instruments and making appropriate adjustments to valves, temperature controls, etc; in a factory, it may be the interval between managers requesting certain information and receiving it.

The selection of the data communications method to be used is also dictated by the required response time. Depending on the volumes of data it may be decided that manual methods of transmission are the most cost-effective.

The type of file handling device required will also be influenced by response time. Random access units are usually chosen where a fast response is required.

It is possible to examine the various available system configurations to work out the cost of having different response times. However, the true value of the different response times should be also considered. This is more difficult because so many intangibles are involved. It is not easy to put a monetary value on customer satisfaction, up-to-date management information, or the ability to respond promptly to market demands.

Figure 6.1 shows a typical variation in the cost of a system with different response times. A typical pay-off curve is also given.

In some applications the value of having a fast, or real-time response is only marginally better than that of a slow response. In other applications a fast response time is vital, ie a computerised system without fast response time would not be viable. This is particularly true when the public is directly involved, for example an on-line aircraft booking system where passengers wishing to check-in must be dealt with in a few minutes.

The various functions carried out by different parts of a total system often need different response times, and Figure 6.1 is therefore an over-simplification. The systems analyst must determine the response time required by each of the various functions of the system. To take further the aircraft booking example quoted above; fast response time is required on passenger enquiries but a slower turnaround of airline statistics and reports is acceptable.

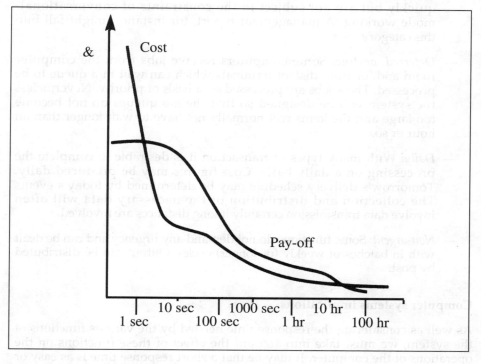

Figure 6.1   Cost vs response time and pay-off

Types of response time

The most common response time requirements may be divided up into the categories shown below:

— *Immediate*: Systems controlling a technical process may need to give a very fast response to certain events. A switch closing or a temperature being exceeded may cause an immediate interruption of the program being run. A program to deal with the condition is executed to give the fastest response possible.

— *Conversational*: People may be using the computer in a conversational manner. Examples include answering enquiries, making an airline booking, debugging a program, or processing a bank transaction. In these cases, the response time must be geared to human reaction time. Less than one second is unnecessarily fast and may be intimidating More than ten seconds is too long, and the human terminal operator will become impatient. If the operator is carrying on a complex conversation with a computer, the response needs to be within two or threeseconds Users of a terminal judge the performance of the entire system from the response which they themselves obtain, even though the computer may well be concurrently processing many tasks. This must be taken into account when meeting users' requirements.

— *Convenient*: Some terminal-based transactions may require to be processed quickly but are not subject to the constraints of conversational-mode working. A management report, for instance, might fall into this category.

— *Deferred, on-line:* Some computers receive jobs from the computer room and/or from distant terminals which can wait in a queue to be processed. These jobs are processed on a basis of priority. Nevertheless the system will be designed so that the job queues do not become too large and the items will normally not have to wait longer than an hour or so.

— *Daily:* With many types of transaction it is desirable to complete the processing on a daily basis. Cost figures may be produced daily. Tomorrow's delivery schedule may be determined by today's events The collection and distribution of the necessary data will often involve data transmission certainly if long distances are involved.

— *Non-urgent:* Some functions do not demand any urgency and can be dealt with in batches of weekly (or longer) cycles. Output can be distributed by post.

Computer systems implications

As well as considering the response time needed by the various functions of the system, we must take into account the effect of these functions on the operations of the computer. It may be that a short response time is as easy or as inexpensive to achieve as a longer one, but generally it will prove more difficult.

Real-time systems will usually have to meet fluctuating demands with peaks of traffic at certain times of the day. A bank, for instance, may have a lunch-time peak of activity whilst a hospital outpatient system will have peaks of patient arrivals at the beginning of the morning and afternoon sessions. Other systems may have momentary peaks of transactions lasting only a few seconds when many terminal operators happen to use the system at the same moment. If the system is to be designed to meet these peaks without any undue degradation in response time, then a faster processor and/or storage media will be required, than in a level demand situation. If the peaks can be flattened in some way, perhaps by delaying some transactions on a priority basis, then a more economic system may be employed.

A fast response to random transactions may require larger immediate access storage and faster hardware. If a slower response can be tolerated, transactions needing the same program can be queued and processed as a block. This will depend upon the variation in transaction types.

Again, if transactions are processed at random, the access time on the random files will be fairly long. If the transactions are queued, it may be possible to reduce the access time by processing together transactions which relate to a given part of the file.

Systems with a high throughput of real-time transactions need a sophisticated supervisory program to control their actions. This may allow many simultaneous seeks and file references and involve a high degree of multiprogramming. With such a supervisory program the system may give a response time of a second or two unless it becomes seriously overloaded. Often in such a system a response time of ten seconds is no less expensive than one of two seconds.

A smaller system may process only one real-time item at a time. Here, the queueing of transactions, giving a slower response, may be of value in increasing the total throughput of the system or allowing it to perform more non real-time work.

When different transactions need different response times, a means of allocating priorities of processing is needed. This is a standard function of the supervisory programs. A system may be handling a job stream of items for low-priority processing, for which a response time of an hour is adequate, and at the same time dealing with urgent items needing a fast response. All the transactions arrive via the transmission lines. The low-priority ones are put in the job queue, and the urgent ones are lined up for immediate processing.

The required response time for similar transactions may vary with the originating location. It is often too expensive to give all user- points an on-line terminal. A bank, for example, may put terminals in its main branches but not in its smaller ones.

The small branches must keep their own customer records or telephone a location with a terminal to obtain information.

A study of the data flow needed within an organisation for its computer system must place different response-time values on different functions and different locations. These will be determined by economics and by the mechanisms needed for control.

Two types of approach have been used in commercial data processing: batch processing and on-line processing. However, due to rapid technological developments, improvements in telecommunications and a dramatic reduction in hardware costs, we now have a much wider variety of systems options.

These are discussed in this chapter under the following headings:

— batch processing

— on-line systems

— real-time systems

— distributed computing

— small business systems

— office automation.

6.3 BATCH PROCESSING

This is the original method of data processing and may in some circumstances still be the best solution. However, the methods of data capture and subsequent transmission of output are more sophisticated than those employed originally. Furthermore, the batch processing is likely to be carried out in a mixed environment where on-line systems take priority and batch processing is performed in the "background".

Characteristics

The characteristics of batch processing are the same:

— large volumes of data

— turnaround times which are not critical

— a whole series (suite) of programs which processes one set of data

— the complete set of data is passed through each program in turn

— processing efficiency is considered to be more important than rapid turnaround of results

— the system processes data at a rate which is determined by the computer — not the operator.

An obvious feature is delay, with the possibility that this may decrease the value of the data.

The elements of a batch processing cycle are:

— data capture (traditionally handwritten documents)

— data transmission (by vehicle or transmission line as in remote-job entry)

— transcription or data-entry (usually key-to-tape/disk), with verification

— job assembly by the data control section

— computer processing

— job disassembly

— distribution of results (again by physical transport of paper or by data transmission in the case of remote-job entry).

Data volumes tend to be large and held for some (often lengthy) period of time. This means allocating a significant amount of back storage to the file.

Figure 6.2   Batch processing elements

The most common tasks are in sorting, merging and updating files in serial fashion by running the transaction file alongside the previous master file. This may be considered "old-fashioned" but is in fact the most efficient use of CPU time, as jobs are not constantly being interrupted, as in a real-time system. Examples of applications suited to batch processing are payroll, invoicing, statements and accounting routines.

Batch processing methods are also still used (in otherwise more sophisticated systems) for housekeeping routines, security dumping, etc.

Remote batch systems

These systems involve batch processing at the central computing facility, but the physical transportation of input and output documents is replaced by data communications. At the user (remote) end, a remote-job entry terminal with a line printer is used to perform the input/output functions.

Jobs are entered at the terminal; data is transmitted to the central computer and held for subsequent processing. Results are written to a file before being transmitted back over the telecommunication lines.

This method of working is sometimes also classified as an on-line system but since it lacks any conversational element, it falls more logically into the batch system category.

6.4 ON-LINE SYSTEMS

Characteristics

As discussed in the introduction to this chapter, a fast response time often demands the implementation of an on-line system.

The on-line system with its conversational element offers many other advantages in addition to fast response time. Validity checks can be made on transactions at the time they are entered, and mistakes picked up immediately while the terminal operator is in contact. The terminal can be used either for enquiries or for communicating with the computer. The computer may process the transaction and check for any exceptional conditions that the operator may be able to correct. For example, the customer's credit status may be checked. The operator may then be given the option to accept an order, despite an unsatisfactory credit position, or to have that order put on a rejected list to be reported later.

There are a number of devices used for communicating with an on-line system. The most common are visual display units with typewriter-style keyboards, but in some applications, specialised terminals may be used. These include terminals which can accept the input of a customer's savings bank passbook or an airline passenger's passport.

Various input and output devices are dealt with in more detail in Chapter 2.

Transmission lines must be chosen to meet the required response times and data volumes of the terminals, and the available facilities are described in Chapter 3.

Figure 6.3 illustrates a possible on-line system. The main plant computer receives data or enquiries directly from its terminals. It will answer enquiries almost immediately, but may stack other data on file to await processing. A data collection system is also on-line to the computer, providing up to the minute shop-floor data for production scheduling, enquiries and so on. A remote subsidiary factory has a small computer system independent of the main plant system. (See also "distributed computing" later in this section). Overnight, the small computer transmits details of plant output, raw material requirements and other needs, and shipments made, to the main plant over a dial-up line. It receives the up-to-date manufacturing plan, depot stock levels and similar data in return.

The next day, the small computer continues its control operations taking the new demands and other details into account. Similarly, the main plant system

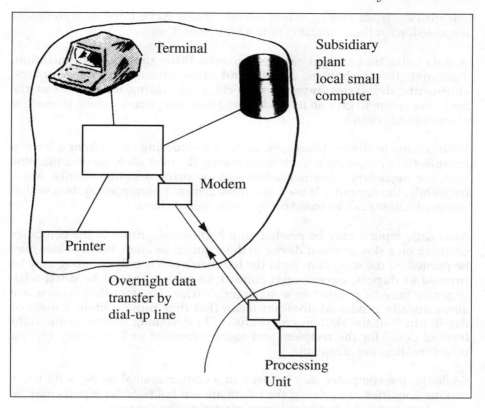

Figure 6.3 On-line system

records the data received and processes it as though it had come from one of the branch terminals. This offers an acceptable service to the remote subsidiary and the main plant at a very low cost, compared to the cost of dedicated data transmission lines, when no particularly rapid response is needed nor could be utilised by the remote plant.

Data collection systems

Many companies entered the field of data communications via a factory data collection system. Following successful applications such as payroll, invoicing, accounts, etc the computer department studied the production aspects of the business. It was discovered that data was often out of date and sometimes inaccurate. To rectify this, terminals were installed on the shop floor to improve the immediacy of data collection.

Data collection can be on-line or off-line; in the latter case, data is collected for later processing. The shop-floor terminals can be card readers, badge readers, paper-tape readers, or special data-collection devices. Robust and easy-to-use keyboards and numeric entry devices have been built to be operated by workers. Often the data transmission is uni-directional, ie terminal to computer only. The terminals are used for reporting facts such as when jobs are started or completed, what goods have been received or dispatched or withdrawn from stores, when certain items have been completed or inspected, what the availability of machine tools is, etc.

A data collection system can be scattered throughout an organisation. Terminals in warehouses, depots, and sales offices may report orders, shipments, deliveries, inventory levels, etc building up records at the computer centre to give an up-to-date and accurate picture, which is used for planning and control.

With relatively simple processes, such as re-ordering stock from a known manufacturer or issuing a work ticket stating the next job to go on a machine tool, the necessary documentation may be printed automatically. More frequently, the computer is used as a management information system so that human decisions can be based on up-to-the-minute facts.

Automatic reports may be printed on a high-speed printer at the computer centre or on a slower speed device at the required location. Work tickets may be printed on the shop floor or in the foreman's office; bills of lading may be printed at depots; exceptional conditions which should be dealt with urgently may be printed in a manager's office. The fact that reports are automatically produced does not mean that they must contain a mass of detail. Much of the skill an analyst has is in designing reports at the right level of detail for the recipient and using exception and summary reports wherever these are acceptable.

Secondly, the computer may be used in a conversational mode, with users making enquiries or updating the information it holds. Short reports may be printed on demand, often based on terms defined by the user.

The major advantage of factory data collection is that accurate, up-to-date information should be available to all users — the key factor being that they all see the same information. Centralising data in this way has the advantages of:

— reducing duplication in data collection. If a data-collection system is used, its value is enhanced if it serves as many departments as possible

— reducing duplication in records kept. A compact file organisation can be designed that serves all departments and minimises file reference times and reconciliation of data held in multiple files

— ensuring that decisions are based on a more complete set of information.

In a very large organisation it may be more difficult to cut across departmental lines. Centralisation of the files does not necessarily imply centrally controlled processing, provided that local on-line facilities are available.

On-line systems functions

Some of the major functions which an on-line system can offer include:

— The integration of separate functions, decisions and files. This integration, with the use of databases, provides a common up-to-date picture of the situation available to all users. This has implications on security and recovery requirements, but the overall advantages of savings in file duplication and file compatibility are considerable.

— Centralisation of information. Many organisations have their factories, distribution depots and offices spread over large distances, often in several countries. An on-line computer system can offer the company the flexibility to enjoy the advantages associated with both a centralised or local computer system. This is expanded later in this chapter under the heading of *Distributed Computing*.

— Fast information services. Examples of this are police records, library systems, banking and stock availability.

— Efficient data collection. The efficiency of data collection can be improved by using an on-line system. Data input conversationally by the user with corrections being made "in flight". Data collection terminals may allow the input of batches of data from remote sites without physical movement. Direct input of data through connection of the plant to the computer is also possible.

— Information routeing. Dissemination of information is a problem in all organisations. Many companies have installed message switching systems or electronic mail systems to enable messages to be sent from person to person or broadcast to several individuals or departments. These are dependent on on-line facilities and are discussed later in this chapter.

— Fast turnaround time. This is a major advantage in multi-user situations where batch processing was previously used. Typical examples in this category are the time-sharing systems discussed later in the chapter.

— Use of a distant computer. More users can be given access to computing facilities than are justified on a stand-alone basis at remote sites. Communications links may offer facilities for back-up arrangements if one part of the computing system breaks down.

6.5   REAL-TIME SYSTEMS

Characteristics

Real-time systems are by definition on-line systems with tighter constraints on response time and availability. In these systems the data is processed to make results available within a timescale which can influence external events, either automatically as in a process control system, or via a human user.

The term "real-time" therefore covers several types of system which respond differently according to environmental needs. Note that in its narrower sense of control, automation and monitoring the system normally responds within a fraction of a second and involves input/output devices linked directly to the computer.

Characteristics of real-time systems include:

— a small volume of data is involved at any one time

— urnaround is critical

— processing efficiency is subordinate to response need

— the system responds to and often controls its environment, so feedback is essential and processing must keep pace with external events

— high availability is required.

Examples of real-time systems include control of a chemical process in which the computer scans instruments and sets pressures, temperatures, and flows to their optimum value. Other examples are the routeing of work through a factory, control of the sequence of operations in a changing situation, even the control of traffic flow through a city by altering traffic lights at peak periods.

Time-sharing systems

Most real-time systems with manually operated terminals are time shared, meaning that more than one user can use them at the same time. When the machine pauses in the processing of one user's item, it switches to another user.

The term time-sharing, however, is commonly used to refer to a system in which the users are independent, each using the terminal as though it were the console of his own computer and entering, testing, and executing programs of his own at the terminal. The work or programs of one terminal user are quite unrelated to the work or programs of other users.

6.6 DISTRIBUTED COMPUTING

Definition

The essential requisites for a system to be described as "distributed" may be summarised as:

— siting of computer processing ability at more than one location

— application of that ability to user-oriented tasks

— interconnection of the locations, and hence use of some data transmission facility

— some element of data handling (not necessarily data storage) at each location

— conformity to common standards for the conduct of operations.

The following definition can be considered:

A distributed system is one in which there are several autonomous but interacting processors and/or data stores at different geographical locations.

Such a definition requires several qualifications. Distributed data handling need not imply full scale updating of stored files, but might include a relatively ancillary task, eg compilation of a validated input file. Thus key-to-storage data preparation with an on-line transfer capability would be admissible in this context.

Similarly, where the amount of data handling is minimal, satellite devices with processing power, but without backing storage peripherals, might also be defined as "distributed".

A distinction must be drawn between distributed systems and distributed processors. Processing units are now available which have been built up from a number of small computers physically adjacent and interconnected by cable. Typically such a multi-processor configuration may have a specialist small computer handling communications, another arranging access to stored files and yet others to undertake arithmetic and memory tasks.

The distinction should also be drawn between distributed and networking systems. In networking systems the objective is to transport tasks efficiently to an optimum processing resource which is not usually sited at the point of user activity. By contrast, the objective of distributed systems is to process as many tasks as economically possible or administratively desirable, at the point of user activity.

Networking takes the job to the processing resource; distribution takes the processing resource to the user. Local area networks fall anywhere between these two extremes.

The intelligent terminal

The evolution of distributed systems has been heavily influenced by the emergence of intelligent terminals (now mainly microcomputers) which can act either as the local processing device or as the user interface in a resource sharing network.

Terminals are the interface between an on-line computing system and the user of its information. Physically they are at the end of a communications line, but from a human viewpoint they are part of the computer.

When minicomputers were relatively expensive, it was economically and operationally advantageous to group a number of terminals around a small computer whose power was shared between all the terminals in the cluster. Such terminals could not be described as "intelligent" since their processing ability was entirely devoted to machine functions.

As minicomputers and microprocessors have become more powerful, and much less expensive, a point has been reached at which small processors can be incorporated into each terminal. Thus the equipment at the point of user activity does not only handle the central communications requirements but can also process a number of user tasks. This is the class of terminal generally described as "intelligent".

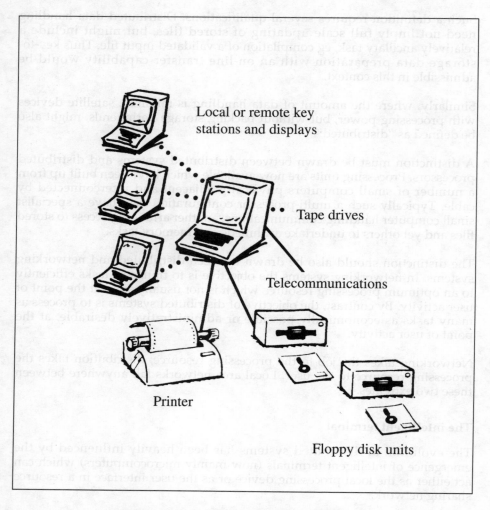

Local or remote key stations and displays

Tape drives

Telecommunications

Printer

Floppy disk units

Figure 6.4 Intelligent terminal system

Classification of distributed systems

A broad classification of distributed systems may be made on the basis of scale of equipment, network configuration and application of remote intelligence, as described below.

Small computer-based systems
These configurations involve linking one or more small computers sited at points of user activity to a significantly larger (or maxi) mainframe (or host) computer to which particular tasks are passed.

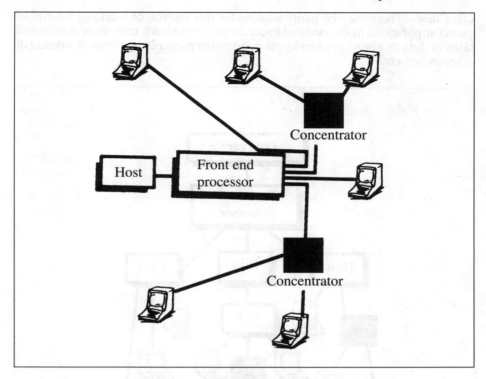

Figure 6.5   Centralised/small computer system

Multi-tier systems
These effectively fall within the small computer systems described but involve more than two sizes of equipment.

Such systems are centred on a principal host (or hosts), often supported by a front-end processor and possibly by regional concentrators, primarily for data communication purposes. At the lowest level is a mixture of terminals, some intelligent and some unintelligent. The intelligent terminals may themselves support a sub-network of keyboards, sensors or other data-gathering devices. In between, and linked both up and down the hierarchy, are other systems, perhaps performing some regional role. These devices may be micro, mini or maxi, depending upon the context of the application.

A multi-tier system has intelligent terminals which incorporate microprocessors to perform minimal user tasks, such as editing and validation, linked to medium-sized computers to process the major user applications. These in turn are linked to one or more large mainframes which gather administrative information of corporate interest and provides an in-house bureau service for specialist applications.

Multi-mini system
The grid situation described above involves minicomputers at points of user activity, which process some user applications locally and refer other tasks to

other hosts. There may be many reasons for this referral of work, eg referral of prime applications in the event of breakdown or overload, transfer of nominated tasks or data to a headquarters location, access to particular facilities at a centre of competence, etc.

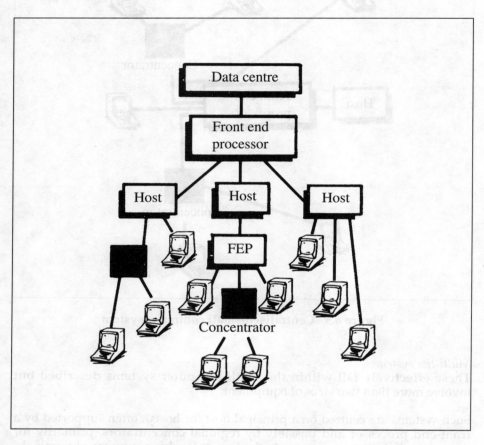

Figure 6.6   Multi-tier system

Resource sharing
The major objective here is to share data and peripherals, either for stand-by purposes or in order to provide centres of specialisation. These systems may assume the configurations of maxi-mini or multi-mini. The ARPA network in the United States is a prime example of resource sharing in the scientific field. This system it is an extensive grid interconnecting many hosts, each offering different specialist facilities.

Application areas of distributed computing

Dedicated (or prime) application. Major examples being sales order processing, data entry, interrogation of locally held files for inventory control, broking, reservation, etc.

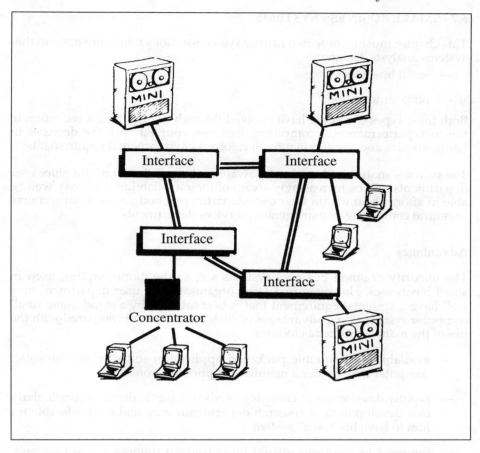

Interface

Interface

Interface

Interface

Concentrator

MINI

MINI

Figure 6.7   Multi-mini system

Data gathering, eg point of sale, process control, shop floor data recording, telemetry, etc. Data gathering usually includes some pre -processing such as first level validation, format conversion, or data compression, together with reporting of error conditions and audit control.

Data dissemination, eg remote printing of warehouse documentation, invoices and statements, sales or production analyses, etc. Data dissemination may be accomplished with minimal employment of the intelligence of remote sites but this usually generates a significant overhead in the central processor. It is not necessary for the remote equipment to be attended at all times.

Where an application is dominated by output volume and where the "corporate reaction time" (the elapsed time before a person takes action on a report) can be defined in terms of hours rather than minutes, it is usually more economic to employ batch transmission, possibly with auto-answer equipment at the terminals. Where the corporate reaction time may be defined in minutes, the use of remote intelligence to control a sub-network of printing devices may be justified.

6.7　SMALL BUSINESS SYSTEMS

This chapter must include two further systems options which are open to the systems analyst/designer:

— small business systems

— office automation.

Both these types of system have evolved through the significant reduction in the cost/performance of computing facilities, coupled with the decrease in hardware size and the elimination of rigorous environmental requirements.

The systems analyst will need to be aware of these systems options since user departments will be increasingly aware of their availability, and may well be able to afford them within their own departmental budgets without recourse to central computing or management services departments.

Advantages

The majority of small business systems are, as the name implies, used in small businesses. However, in a large organisation, a user department may well have a systems requirement that is best satisfied by a stand-alone small computer system. Some advantages of such a solution are compared with the use of the main computer as follows:

— availability of suitable packaged application software for the small computer may render a mainframe option uneconomic

— rapidly developing or changing needs of a particular user (particularly in a development or research department) may make it preferable for him to have his "own" system

— the need to connect unusual input/output devices at the user end, which are best implemented without interruption to the main system

— use of a small computer to prove the feasibility of a system, on a pilot basis, before adoption of the system by the main computing facility

— short-term computing requirements of a user, where it is cheaper and quicker to process locally than to install temporary telecommunications facilities. When the requirement by one user ceases, the small computer can then be moved to another user

— lack of resources, human, computing or telecommunications at the main computing facility mean that user departments needs cannot be met quickly enough

— local processing is the only requirement, and shared files and communications are unnecessary.

Pitfalls

The obvious dangers for an organisation adopting small business computers is to allow the user departments to make the same mistakes that have been made in the past by the now established computer profession. It is recommended, therefore, that while the small business computers may be "stand-alone", the user departments should not be left to stand alone. A central policy should be established by the organisation for the procurement and support of such computer systems. This will bring about cost savings through purchasing arrangements producing a re-usable pool of computers. This will create some degree of standardisation to allow interchange of ideas, hardware, software and complete systems.

Whilst it may be desirable for the user department to be free from any constraints imposed by a central department, it is necessary to afford some protection from possible pitfalls. Since the purchase price of small systems are within the budget of many user departments, it is very easy to purchase the system without realising all its future implications.

Here are a few of those potential pitfalls:

— vendors of hardware may not be interested in the user's problems after the sale. It is up to the user to ensure that the hardware purchased will adequately meet his current and planned needs

— even with the increased reliability of integrated circuit technology, breakdowns will occur. It is at this time that the user really tests the quality of support available from his supplier

— computer systems require rational and disciplined clerical procedures to support them. This involves staff training and continuing supervision of the system

— security and general housekeeping routines must be carefully adhered to

— computer systems are not implemented overnight, and the changeover to the system, and its associated data entry requirement, may take several months to achieve.

These are just a few of the problems which may be minimised by drawing on the expertise of the central IT staff.

6.8 OFFICE AUTOMATION

These systems, by their nature, are based on integration of facilities and are therefore unlikely to be implemented by one single part of the organisation. However, the systems analyst may feel that this is not a computing area and does not fall in his range of systems options. This is a narrow view, since the big pay-off in office systems is the integration of text and data through the interconnection of computing and office equipment.

Environment and scope

Today two developments — the microprocessor and telecommunications advances — have created possibilities for information creation, storage, retrieval and movement that have not existed before. For example, microprocessors in voice recognition units are opening the way for speech input of information and microprocessors provide text-editing facilities. Microprocessor-controlled lasers, together with photocopying technology, are providing image printers which are capable of producing, at high speed, sheets of intermixed text and graphic information and retaining the convenience of photocopier capability.

Satellites are now offering information transmission speeds of around seven million bits per second, and developments in the application of fibre-optics offer speeds of 1,000 million bits per second. These advances create opportunities for the development of services which could handle the bulk of current business mail.

Teletex, a modernised version of telex, is now available, and gives the advantages of telex but with higher transmission speeds.

So what needs are there to be satisfied by this new technology? Here are a few:

— rising costs of skilled support staff

— attraction of low cost, high performance automated systems

— reduction in quality of the mail service

— other increasing costs (eg office rental)

— competition

— recognition of the value of information.

Office activity

The total information system of an organisation can be divided into two areas: IT and informal office systems.

Historically, IT deals with the formal side of company information handling, and works to a set of well-defined rules for each application. It presents formal interfaces to its users through forms and procedure manuals and it demands rigorous job training for its operators. IT accepts predictable input and produces predictable output. Changes to these systems are introduced by re-definition and re-specification. Much of this output is essential to company operation, eg invoices, payslips, production schedules.

Informal office systems, on the other hand, operate in the more undefined areas of office activity. Typically they attend to tasks which are performed as required in a manner suitable for that moment. They are systems designed by the user for his own particular purpose. Rules are not entirely absent from informal systems. Common sense and traditional protocols do provide a basis for procedures. Users of such systems require a general skill training rather than the strict job training of IT systems, and changes to informal systems generally occur by evolution.

The boundaries between IT and informal office systems can be hazy and are likely to become more so as more activities are automated. Because the equipment used in automating office systems has derived from the computers used in the widespread automation of IT, it is not surprising that a distinction cannot always be drawn.

The one place where information technology and informal office systems do meet is in the accessing of the company database. The full force of the strict IT systems has created a well-defined corporate database, holding details of the company's operations. This information can then be widely used; it can be referred to in meetings, as a basis for taking decisions; it can be publicised in press releases; and it can be mentioned in warnings about poor productivity.

The informal office

Work in the informal office environment falls into four categories as shown in Figures 6.8 to 6.11.

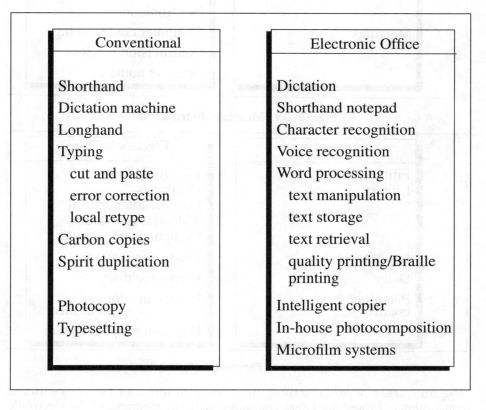

Figure 6.8   Document preparation

It is to these four categories that electronic office technology can be applied, not only to carry out existing tasks more efficiently but also to allow new tasks to be performed.

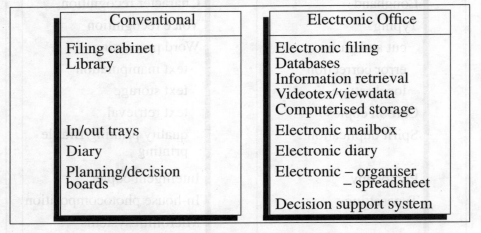

Conventional	Electronic Office
Telephone	Telephone - voice store
Telegram	and forward
	sophisticated
	exchanges
Telex	Telex and Teletex
Courier	Facsimile and hybrid
	OCR/facsimile
Internal mail	Communicating word
	processors
P.O. mail	Prestel message service
	Electronic mail
Meetings	Computer conferencing
	Confravision service
	Office at home

Figure 6.9   Message distribution

Conventional	Electronic Office
Filing cabinet	Electronic filing
Library	Databases
	Information retrieval
	Videotex/viewdata
	Computerised storage
In/out trays	Electronic mailbox
Diary	Electronic diary
Planning/decision boards	Electronic – organiser
	– spreadsheet
	Decision support system

Figure 6.10   Personal information

The four areas of office activity are shown in terms of the conventional constituents of those activities, compared with the elements of the electronic office that may now be used.

Although the four areas are shown separately, there is a great deal of interaction and interdependence. For example, the arrangement and confirmation of a meeting between two people involves all four areas:

— telephone conversation deciding on the meeting

— message distribution

— access and update of diaries to fix a date

— personal information management

— access of train/flight information to fix the time

— information access

Conventional	Electronic Office
Electronic filing	eg Viewdata, eg Prestel
Telephone enquiries Videotex/viewdata	Information broadcast system eg Oracle/Ceefax (teletext)
Catalogues/timetables	Touchstone telephone input voice synthesiser output
The media Procedure manuals	Access to computerised information bases
Directories	Company database Microfilm retrieval systems

Figure 6.11   Information access

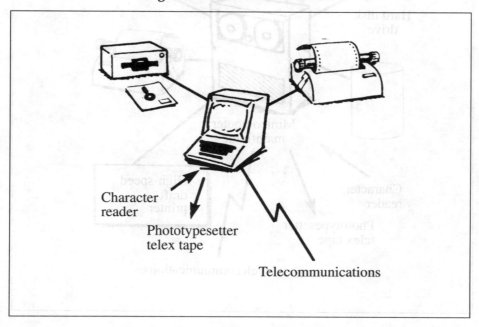

Character reader

Phototypesetter telex tape

Telecommunications

Figure 6.12   Stand-alone office system

- preparation of a letter to confirm the meeting
- despatch of the letter
- registration of the letter. management.

- document preparation
- message distribution
- personal information

Architecture of office systems

Some specific electronic office architectures have been mentioned: the local area network and PBX controlled network. Other architectures which can provide some or all of the necessary facilities are described below. There are many variations possible within and between each described architecture. The four main architectures are:

- stand-alone
- shared resource
- PBX controlled network
- local area network.

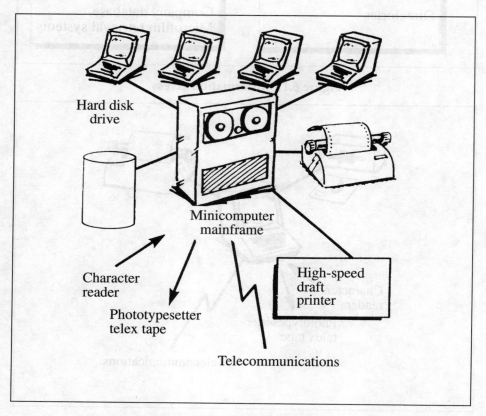

Figure 6.13   Shared resource office system

Stand-alone

This is a term first coined for single workstation word processors. These are capable of operating independently of any other unit, having local processing power, a quality printer, and local storage. Such equipment operating alone can only offer limited electronic office facilities, and it is anticipated that within the next five years, devices without communications facilities will have become obsolete. Capability can be enhanced by using local links to laser printers, phototypesetting and telex terminals and by employing character recognition equipment for the input of typed documents.

Links to a central computer can enhance the storage facilities, provide high-speed, large volume printing and also give access to the corporate database. Communications facilities linking stand-alone devices can provide a document- or message-distribution capability. The stand-alone device could become a workstation on the other architectures to be described, thereby giving a wide range of facilities.

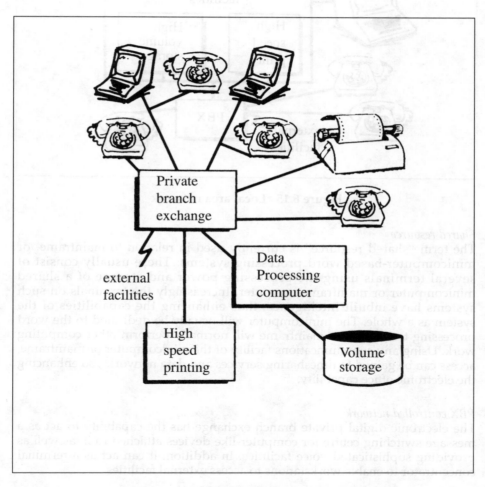

Figure 6.14   PBX controlled office system

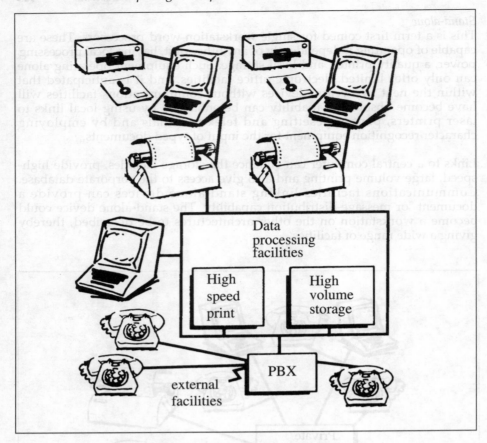

Figure 6.15   Local area network

Shared resource
The term "shared resource" is currently used in relation to mainframe- or minicomputer-based word processing systems. These usually consist of several terminals using the processing power and storage of a shared minicomputer or mainframe computer. Increasingly the terminals on such systems have inbuilt intelligence, thus enhancing the capabilities of the system as a whole. The minicomputer will usually be dedicated to the word processing task, whilst a mainframe will normally perform other computing work. Using any communications facility of the minicomputer or mainframe, access can be gained to timesharing services and data networks, so enhancing the electronic office capability.

PBX controlled network
The electronic digital private branch exchange has the capability to act as a message switching centre for computer-like devices attached to it, as well as providing sophisticated voice facilities. In addition, it can act as a terminal concentrator to enable workstations to access external facilities.

As a message switching centre, it can control the routeing of data or text from workstations, and use the IT computer printing and storage facilities. As a terminal concentrator, it can act as an interface to both private and public networks (including the public switch telephone network, packet switch service, telex and Prestel). This type of local network can be established utilising the existing internal telephone network of an organisation, thereby minimising installation costs, whilst providing access to the network wherever a telephone handset currently exists.

Local area network
This architecture provides an alternative to the use of an electronic PBX. It consists of a data highway along which all information flows and to which all devices are connected. The main advantage of this system over other architectures is that it offers simple "plug in the wall" connections. This loop is easily controlled, some degree of device independence is forced by the standard interface, and it offers high speed communications.

Additionally, the potential bottleneck of the PBX or computer controlling conventional networks is removed. In a new site, the laying of a loop of wire gives low installation costs, but in an existing office complex the laying of such a wire could involve building work and therefore such cost advantages may not exist.

As fast as new features of OA, supported by a LAN, are provided, users want more. The plethora of functions which together make up OA, mean that it has moved on from the "office of the future" image which it had not long ago, to a generally accepted way of supporting not only "general manager" but also "general office" applications. Today, the automated office will have the selection of features and facilities which are useful. For example, an office to which large reports or texts are produced will probably have a high resolution display and micro attached to the local network which support the following:

— word processing, with either a local printer or the facility to direct printed output to a suitable printer on the network

— a modem to one of the public networks allowing access to worldwide reference databases, and also allowing access to external electronic mailboxes

— desktop publishing software which can import word processed text and graphics, the latter probably scanned by appropriate equipment somewhere on the network, with the ability to direct output in draft form, or direct to a laser printer, again probably somewhere else on the network

— a local messaging and bulletin board facility

— a meeting arrangement facility allowing access to the "diaries" of all relevant people on the network, enabling meetings to be set-up whether people are at their desk or not

— access to an in-house database, allowing retrieval of work previously written, and any similar information.

By contrast, a sales office would probably have a different set of facilities, and these might include:

— read-only access to current orders and the main computer, via the LAN

— read-only access to the current sales catalogue information

— access to the names and addresses and order history from the customer file on the main computer

— an order input facility, allowing orders to be placed

— word processing, probably with a local printer

— modem link to an external network, probably including a "fax" facility, both sending and receiving

— local messaging and diary functions as above.

Someone working from home, either alone or as a remote outstation to their office, may have no more than a general purpose micro and printer, with appropriate software and a modem.

These kinds of application are now common, and have taken their proper place as tools, rather than technological marvels. Nevertheless, they have had to be designed and implemented. This has involved selection from what is available, as well as forward planning to allow what is becoming available to be added when it is seen to be appropriate. Any of the OA facilities, whether or not they include use of a LAN, or the high speed data communications systems currently available, represent a considerable investment in hardware, software and training.

6.9 CONCLUSION

The options available to the systems designer are wide ranging. In most cases there will be more than one viable solution to the user's requirements. The designer must therefore be aware of the variety of choice offered and the implications not only on the immediate processing needs of the user but also on future developments.

The stand-alone system, for instance, may solve an immediate problem but limit future developments which require data communications. By selecting a device to which communications facilities can be added, such a problem can be avoided.

Compatibility between systems is also important. There is nothing more annoying than having data on one system and not being able to access it from another system.

This chapter has outlined most of the available options but the designer needs to consider the pros and cons of each type in a given situation in order to provide the user with the best value for money solution.

NOW TRY THESE...

1. Distinguish carefully between the three processing modes: batch, on-line, interactive.

2. Discuss the factors which influence the choice of processing mode for the following systems:

    (a) An enquiry system for a life assurance company

    (b) An order processing system for a mail order company

7 Data organisation

OBJECTIVES

When you have worked through this chapter, you should be able to:

— outline the purpose of master, transaction, work, security and audit files and how they differ

— describe the hierarchical nature of a file in terms of sub-files, records and data elements (field)

— briefly explain the use of key and index fields

— state the nature, advantages and disadvantages of fixed and variable length records and fields

— explain the value of blocking data

— describe the four main types of file organisation as regards tape and disk storage.

INTRODUCTION

The design of a system takes the logical requirements specified by the analyst and turns them into a physical system. Part of this logical to physical conversion involves the transformation of logical data stores into physical data stores. Chapter 2 of this book described the basic backing storage devices available. This chapter considers ways to arrange the data on these devices so that people can later retrieve the information.

This chapter looks at the types of files present in a system and their structure. It considers the structure of records and how to determine file sizes. We look at various file access methods and how to deal with overflows. It concludes with a brief review of file access timings.

A file is:

A collection of items of data organised into records in such a way that specific items of data or records can be retrieved and accommodated in main storage when required for processing.

A record is a group of related facts stored in separate fields treated as a unit representing, say, a particular transaction. An example of this is the payment of an invoice against goods received. The record of this transaction would probably contain as related items, the supplier's account number, invoice number, and the total amount paid. A collection of similar records constitutes a file, in this case a file of payment transactions. Each record has within it a key field which is used to identify the record.

7.1 TYPE OF FILES

There are five broad categories of data file used in any information system:

— master

— transaction

— work

— security

— audit.

The designer will certainly have to design the first two types. Depending on the system, or the software in use, and (partially) on definitions, he may or may not have to design the other three types.

Master file

A master file is a file that is permanent in the sense that it is never, apart from the time of its creation, empty. The normal means of updating a master file is by adding, deleting or amending records in the file. Master files can be further subdivided into two types:

— static master files (or reference files). The business entities that these files describe are of a permanent or semi-permanent nature (eg products, suppliers, customers, employers, etc)

— dynamic master files. The business entities these files describe are of transitory importance to the business (eg customer orders, work orders, job tickets, projects, etc).

In a sense, the distinction between these two types of file is only a matter of degree. Dynamic files are simply more volatile than static files. Volatility is a measure of the extent to which the file contents change with time.

Volatility can be defined as:

$$\frac{\text{Number of records in a file which are changed}}{\text{Number of records in the file at the base time}} \times 100\%$$

Transaction files

Transaction files are files in which the data relating to business events is recorded, prior to a further stage of processing. This further processing may

be the use of the transaction data to update master files, or the archiving of the transaction for audit purposes. After the transaction file is processed it is usually re-initialised, and further transactions are then recorded in it.
Examples of transaction files are:

— customer's orders for products (to update an order file)

— details of price changes for products (to update a product file)

— details of cash postings to customer accounts (to be held for audit purposes).

Work file

Any other file which is required to enable the processing of business data to be carried out is a work file (excluding files required for security or audit purposes). The designer may or may not have to design such files himself. Examples where he would not be involved in the design would be:

— work files used by system software or utilities such as sort/merge processes

— work files used as intermediate or inter-process files in computer programs at a low-level. The design of these files would be better left to the programming team.

If a file is needed to store data created by one business process, before being used by another business process, then the designer would have to be involved. (These files are sometimes referred to as transfer files). The temporary files which hold information for printing also fall into this category. Here the designer needs to specify the record definitions required to produce the correctly formatted output.

Security files

These files are taken in order to provide back up copies, in case of loss or damage to current versions. The techniques of file security are discussed in Book 6, of the NCC Systems Training Library, *Systems Controls*.

In practice, the designer is unlikely to be involved in the detailed design of such files, as he would rely either on system security software (eg dump/restore utilities; the transaction logging and recovery routines in teleprocessing monitors); or, in batch update systems, in holding superseded versions of master files with back copies of transaction files.

Audit files

Audit files are a particular type of transaction file. They play the same role in computerised information systems as the postings in a traditional manual ledger. They enable the auditor to check the correct functioning of the computer procedures, by storing copies of all the transactions which cause the permanent system files to be altered. For example, in a sales ledger system, the transactions to be recorded might be:

— invoice number, date, cash amount for each invoice raised

— date and amount of cash received

— credit note number, date, amount of money credited

— account adjustment, amount of money, cross-reference to authorisation, adjustment code.

These files will normally be serial, the records being created at the time of the master file update and accumulated, in the sequence of the update, on the audit file.

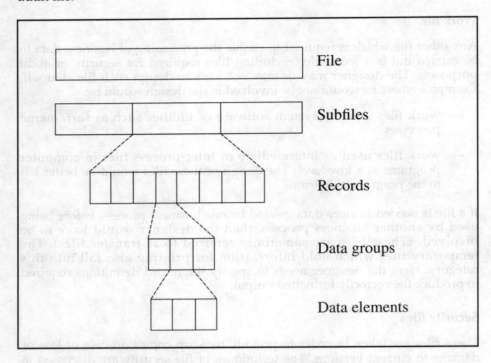

Figure 7.1   Multi-level file structure

7.2   FILE STRUCTURE

Files are multi-level structures, the sub-structures of which are shown in Figure 7.1.

Files and subfiles

A file may consist of various subfiles. In a production control system the parts control master file may contain a series of records for each part manufactured, and each record could be considered to belong to a subfile in its own right, consisting of:

— work-in-progress records detailing operations outstanding

— outstanding parts order records detailing orders outstanding for the specific part

— purchase parts order records where the part is brought out.

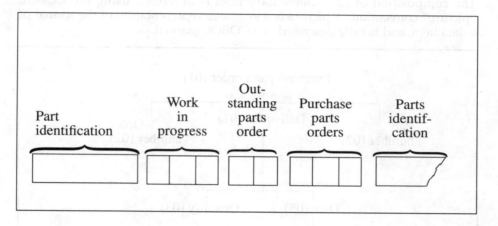

Figure 7.2 File structure

The same logical file structure consisting of a number of logically grouped records, can be physically separated for convenience of handling as shown in Figure 7.2. To save repetition of the same descriptive data for each of the physical records, a header record has been added.

To show the relationships of these records within the file, the hierarchical levels of the family tree can be described by assigning alphabetic letters to each level, starting with the letter A at the highest level.

7.3 RECORD STRUCTURES

Each of the records consists of groups of data called data items, the arrangement and relationships of which combine to form the structure of a particular record. Figure 7.3 shows the data items contained in the purchase order record of Figure 7.2.

It may be necessary to further subdivide some of these items. The lowest level is called an elementary item, or data element and the upper level an item group. One way of denoting these levels is that used in COBOL and PL/1. Each item is allocated a level number; an item at any given level includes all items following it until a level number less than or equal to it is shown. Many levels are possible, but in practice it is unusual to have more than five.

Specifying record structure

A description of the data items contained in each record must be clearly and methodically recorded, eg by means of the NCC standard form S44, *Record Specification* (see Figure 7.4). The sequence in which the items are recorded represents the actual format of the record on its medium. The "position" columns reflect the position of each item within the record, in this example, in bytes.

The composition of each elementary item is described using the COBOL "picture" convention. A picture is a symbolic representation of the format of a data item, and is fully described in a COBOL manual.

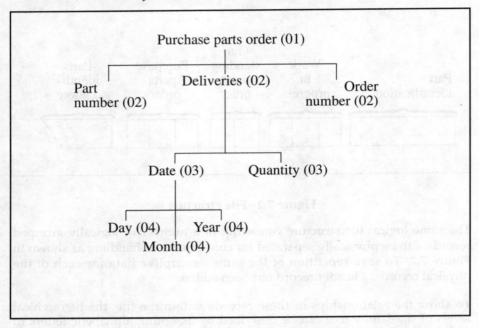

Figure 7.3   Item levels in a record

Each item can be described further by indicating its value as a range (minimum/maximum) or specific characters; this is mainly used for validity checking. An entry in the occurrence column indicates that that particular item occurs more than once, and the identical items are therefore not repeated.

Key field

One or more of the data elements will act as the key field of the record and is used for identifying the record for location and processing purposes. The key field for a particular file is shown on the file specification in our example, the key is the part number. In a sales ledger file, the key field might be the customer code; in a payroll file, the key field might be the employee number.

The term "field", which is sometimes used as a synonym for data element, more specifically defines the space which an item occupies in terms of its data type.

The key field or fields is/are the identifier(s) of the record. Index fields may be the same or different, and are used in relational database working to present the

No	From	To	Length	Name / system design	In program	Data Type	Size	Picture	Occurrence	Value Range
1	01	05	02	Part number		C	5	Z(5)		1-99999
2	06	45	02	Deliveries					5	
3	06	11	03	Delivery date						
4	06	07	04	Day		C	2	9(2)		01-31
5	08	09	04	Month		C	2	9(2)		01-12
6	10	11	04	Year		C	2	9(2)		01-99
7	12	13	03	Quantity		P	2	9(3)		001-999
8	66	60	02	Order number		C	5	X(5)		A0001-A9999

Purchase parts order PC 4.7 PURPRT

Figure 7.4 Form S44, record specification

file to the application program in a desired sequence, which may not be the physical sequence.

Several different indexes can be specified, to enable the file to be presented in different sequences as required, and all direct access updating will automatically update the indexes which are linked to the file at the time. Each index is a separate file, containing basically the record number of the file record plus the value of the index field(s). That file is held in ascending sequence of index field values, and records in the index are moved, inserted or deleted as the file itself is altered. Descending sequence is not needed, because the file can be accessed from the bottom upwards, as well as from the top downwards. A useful aspect of this is not just in the sequence of presentation of the file, but in the access to a specific record. Seeking a record by giving the value of the index field is very rapid, compared to sequential searching! It compares favourably with the more conventional 'indexed sequential' access described later in this chapter.

Naturally, the index file occupies storage space, and the index updating takes time, so the method is particularly valuable when the data records are being updated directly through a keyboard and screen, at the pace of an operator, rather than in "batch mode".

Record length

It is possible to store records in fixed or variable format and length.

Fixed length records

A file is said to consist of fixed length records when each record is the same length. This can be achieved in two ways, either all the records are identical in layout or where the layout is different each record is padded so that the total length is equal to that of the longest. The first is common on most master files whilst the second approach is often found in transaction files where the data required for different transactions varies.

Fixed-length records are usually easier to design and write programs for but can be more wasteful in backing storage than variable-length records.

Variable-length records

There are several types of variable-length record situations (see Figure 7.5); for example:

— a group of different types of record, each of fixed but differing lengths

— records with a fixed minimum length and a variable number of fixed-length items following the fixed portion

— records with a fixed minimum length and a fixed number of variable-length items following the fixed portion

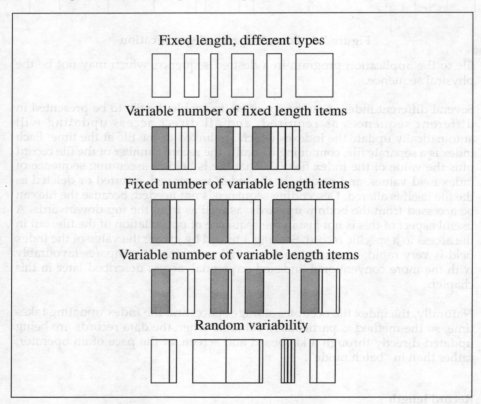

Figure 7.5 Variable length records

— records with a fixed minimum length and a variable number of variable-length items following the fixed portion

— complete and random variability of length.

Often it is possible to break down a variable-length record into a group of fixed-length records, so that with careful design, the advantages of both fixed and variable working can be achieved.

The use of several fixed-length physical records forming one variable-length logical record, can make programming complex. However, it eliminates the necessity to specify the maximum length of a record, and individual records can be processed one at a time, thus making the best use of storage. The production control example falls into this category; the parts control record which was defined as a group record can be considered as the variable-length logical record referring to that part. It has to be variable because the various subfiles (work-in-progress, outstanding orders, etc) can vary in length. However, each individual record in the subfiles can be fixed in length.

Data items may also be fixed or variable in length; variable-length items must have an end of item marker or separator. This is typical of files produced by the programming language BASIC. If there is a variable number of variable-length items, each containing data of the same nature, then not only must each item have an end of item marker, but there must also be a different marker for the end of the group of items.

Transfer time (in seconds) $T = (\frac{N}{R} + BS)/1000$

Transfer time (in seconds) $L = \frac{N}{P} + BG$

where

N	=	number of characters
R	=	nominal transfer rate (kc/s)
B	=	number of blocks
S	=	start/stop time (ms)
P	=	packing density (bpi)
G	=	interblock gap (inches)

Actual transfer rate $= \dfrac{\overline{N}}{1000T}$ kc/s

Figure 7.6 Transfer and tape capacity formulas

7.4 BLOCKING

As described in Chapter 2, data written to tape has to be broken into blocks because of the limited size of main store. To use a tape efficiently, large block sizes are necessary. Figure 7.6 shows the formulae to determine the effect of various block sizes on tape capacity and actual transfer rate.

Figure 7.7 shows the effect of blocking on the time taken to transfer a file containing 320 Kbytes. With a record length of 80 bytes it takes 31 seconds to transfer the file. If the records are blocked in eighths the time taken is reduced to under five seconds.

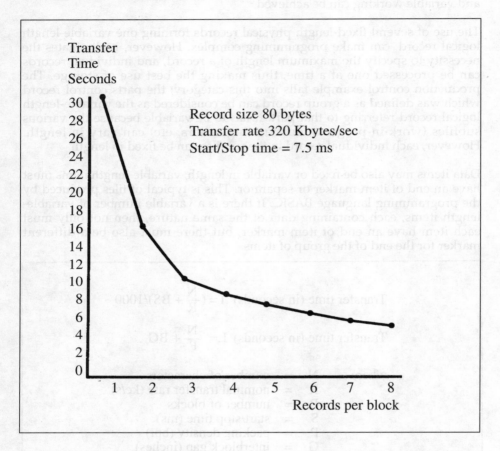

Figure 7.7   Effect of blocking on transfer rate

The block size is influenced not only by the size of each record, but also by whether they are fixed or variable in length. When a file contains only fixed-length records, the block size is normally a multiple of that length; but when a file contains variable-length records, the block size is not less than the expected maximum record length and is normally a multiple of the average length.

There are likely to be other considerations affecting the block size, eg software, constraints on memory, and possibly a standing instruction from management that the size used throughout the installation must not exceed certain minimum and maximum limits (say 1,000 and 2,000 bytes).

7.5 FILE ORGANISATION

The physical organisation of data on backing storage devices (eg magnetic tape or disks) can be defined as the relationship between the values of the key fields on consecutive records and the position on the storage device which they occupy. There are several different ways in which files can be organised, and for each, a separate method of accessing the records must be defined. The choice of organisation method is often a compromise between the requirement for efficient maintenance of files (keeping them up-to-date) and fast retrieval.

The two requirements of efficient maintenance and fast retrieval can be mutually exclusive, though not always: in any particular case, a trade-off must be made between one or the other. It is also generally necessary to achieve a practical balance between storage and processing costs of data. Processing costs can be reduced if the data organisation suits the characteristics and applications of the logical data. Storage costs can sometimes be reduced only at the expense of processing costs.

Files in serial storage

It is important to distinguish between the terms serial and sequential which are sometimes used as though they were synonymous and interchangeable. A serial file is one where each data record is placed in turn in the next available storage space. The record keys need not be in any particular order, and there need be no relationship between the logical position of an item on the file and its physical position on the device. On a serial file, records can only be accessed in the order in which they occur in the given storage medium. This contrasts with sequential file organisation, where records are held and accessed in a pre-determined sequence of keys. The two terms are confused when referring to magnetic tape, which, because it is a serial recording medium, can hold records both serially and sequentially. Paper tape, punched cards and magnetic tape are serial recording media, whereas magnetic disks and optical disks are direct access media.

Basically, files may be organised on serial storage devices in either of two ways:

— randomly, where the records are not held in any particular order: a serial file

— sequentially, with the records held in a pre-determined sequence: a sequential file.

For example, a transaction file of unsorted records held on magnetic tape is a serial file; after sorting the records to a particular key sequence, it becomes a sequentially-organised transaction file.

A serial file has the simplest structure of all methods of file organisation. New records are simply added on to the end of the file. In sequentially-organised serial files (sometimes known as serial sequential files) the records usually follow a certain sequence, according to the ascending (or descending) value of a particular key field in the data record.

It should be noted that sequential files may appear on non-serial media (eg direct access devices such as disks).

Direct access storage

Direct access devices provide an economically feasible compromise between unlimited main store and serial storage devices by providing facilities for:

— storing large amounts of data on-line to the computer

— accessing quickly any given piece of data on the file

— transferring this data at high speed.

Direct access devices comprise:

— exchangeable and fixed disk;

— "floppy" disks

— optical disks.

These all have facilities which are not available on serial storage devices. On disks, for example:

— the read/write heads can traverse the whole extent of the device in a very short time

— each block of data can be directly addressed and accessed by the hardware

— the constant rotational speed is sufficiently accurate to allow the overwriting of individual blocks.

These facilities offer four different methods of organising files:

— serial

— sequential

— indexed sequential

— "random".

Serial organisation
A serial file on disk is identical in structure to a serial file on tape. It is created by placing each record in turn in the next available storage space, leaving no gaps, apart from non-data areas between records. Records are entered in the sequence in which they are presented and no regard is paid to keys. The number of records stored at a single address is called a "bucket" or "page". Pages are fully packed, although records are not split across page boundaries and therefore, packing density may not be 100 per cent. Since there is no structuring, no room is left for insertion and updating is achieved by copying.

This type of organisation is not suitable for master files on direct access devices where it is necessary to insert key records into an existing sequence, or where access by address generation techniques is employed, as there is no overflow facility. It is suitable for:

— transaction files

— print files

— dump files

— files where data is held temporarily.

The advantage of serial organisation is the maximum utilisation of space on the device. In normal use these files are processed from beginning to end and sequence is not important. So, although the theoretical time to find a specific record is, on average, half the total time to search the whole file, the real access time is much faster because the record required is always the next one on the physical device.

Sequential organisation

By definition, sequential files must be structured and stored in a certain sequence of a particular key item or group of items; it must be possible to access records by determining their location from the keys which identify them. The logical sequence of the records need not necessarily be the physical sequence. For example, if certain records in a logical sequence are displaced into overflow areas, they are no longer physically contiguous with the preceding and following logical records. However, they must still be retrieved in sequence. This method combines the advantages of a sequential file with the possibility of random access.

Sequential organisation is suitable for most master files in a normal batch processing environment. It is not normally used for fast-response on-line enquiry systems.

Indexing

For each record on the disk, an index entry is held giving the key of the record and its location on the disk unit. To facilitate searching, the index itself is held in the key sequence, although the actual records need not be. To locate a record, the index must be searched to find the key required and, thereby, the location of the record.

To make an insertion, it is necessary to create a new index entry and insert this into the correct place in the sequential index. This process can take some time. After several runs of the job when several insertions have built up, it is advisable to arrange the index back into sequential order, to improve the efficiency of retrieval.

This basic index method has the disadvantage of requiring large indexes and correspondingly high search times before a record is located, particularly if the index itself is held on the disk. For this reason, it is not very often used. If, however, a high activity portion of the file could be incorporated into the index, eg items of stock balances which change most frequently, the majority of accesses to the main file could be saved.

"Random" organisation

A randomly-organised file contains records stored without regard to the sequence of their key fields. It is created by loading records in any convenient sequence. They are then retrieved by establishing a direct relationship between the key of the record and its address on the file. This can be achieved either by use of an "index" or by "key transformation" to give the address of the record on the file.

"Random" files show a distinct advantage where:

— hit rate is low (ie the number of records accessed in any processing run is small)

— data cannot be batched or sorted

— fast response is required.

It is therefore the usual method of file organisation for on-line, fast-response systems. Further advantages are that insertion and deletion of records is straightforward. Deletion of records provides gaps in the file which can be used for the insertion of later records; alternatively insertions can be made at the end of the file.

It is usual to update files on direct access devices by overwriting existing data. At the same time there must be some provision for additions, and preferably some means of re-utilising storage arising from deletions.

Overflow can arise from:

— a record being assigned to an address which is occupied by another record

— a record being expanded so that it can no longer be accommodated in its present ("home") area.

Overflow may be caused in a sequential file by attempting to insert a record into its correct key sequence but there being no physical space available at that point.

Overflow in a "random" file can be caused by attempting to store more records than a given storage area can accommodate, or, in the case of key transformation, by the existence of a synonym (ie where more than one key is transformed to the same address). There are three basic methods of catering for expansion:

— specifying less than 100 per cent page packing density

— specifying less than 100 per cent disk cylinder packing density

— specifying overflow pages.

To cover the possibility of very irregular expansion in the short-term, an area may be reserved for second-level or independent overflow. This area is reserved as a number of pages which are used as required, when all other overflow facilities have been exhausted.

7.6 CONCLUSION

The principles of data organisation need to be understood by the analyst and designer so that the data can be stored efficiently and retrieved rapidly. The use of tape files is ideally suited to serial file processing. It is cheap and fast. It also provides a good back-up medium for security purposes.

The use of disks permits random access to data which is essential for most on-line processing. However, care must be taken to ensure that the required data can be readily accessed and that processing is not delayed by having too many records to read or write.

This chapter has been concerned mainly with data organisation and access where the mechanisms are under the direct control of the programmer. The advent of database management systems (DBMS) and fourth generation languages (4GLs) has taken some of this control away from the design and development team. The actual mechanisms are handled by standard software. Nevertheless, the principles of organisation and access are just as important because, without care and comprehension, systems designed using DBMS and 4GLs can use very large amounts of backing storage, and can require so many disk accesses to update data files and linked index files that the system is degraded to such an extent that user response time targets are not met.

NOW TRY THESE...

1. Describe in detail the pros and cons of fixed length records and fields.

2. Explain with care the advantages of an electronic data base over the corresponding paper one, using either a library or an office, for example.

3. How would you sort a dropped bundle of library index cards into alpha order of authors? Now make notes on how computers sort records.

4. Outline the arrangement of logical records in a serial access file on tape, and in sequential, indexed sequential and direct access files on disk. Discuss the pros and cons.

5. Describe how a computerised mail order firm would handle its transactions. Start with a list of possible transaction types.

6. From time to time certain parts of a computer system may fail. On one such occasion, the disk controller fails, causing the loss of a file with the day's transactions. Discuss the steps that should have been taken to reduce the possibility of loss of vital data.

7. A library computer system uses two disk files: the book file and the transaction file. During the day the staff use the book file to provide information for staff and users about the books and their availability; at the same time the transaction file is built up; this consists of details of books borrowed and returned, and of new books acquired by the library that day. At night the system uses the transaction file to update the book file.

(a) Make any assumptions you think fit to describe the structures of the files

(b) What precautions should be taken to minimise the danger of losing either of them?

(c) Describe in outline what happens in the nightly run. During this processing, why should the system hold the updating file on a different disk from the main file?

8 People and computers

OBJECTIVES

When you have worked through this chapter, you should be able to:

— outline how a firm's computing (data processing) department relates to other departments

— explain why computers are essential for many firms to survive

— state the value of international computer networks and communications

— show the hierarchical nature of a typical, large data processing department, and outline the work of each person or group

— state what systems and systems analysis mean

— outline the characteristics of a good systems analyst

— describe the states of setting up a new IT-based system

— explain the system life cycle concept

— outline the work of a programmer

— discuss the steps of program development and maintenance

— list likely future developments in information technology

— discuss the advantages and disadvantages of aspects of new IT with regard to society and the individual

— outline the optimistic and pessimistic views of the impact of IT on employment

— state examples of computer-based crime.

INTRODUCTION

It is sometimes easy to forget that computers are tools for people — not the other way round. Computers should make people's work easier, and we have seen in this book a number of ways in which that happens.

Computers create jobs too: a large firm or government department with a large complex computer system may employ hundreds or thousands of people to work with it. In this chapter we start by looking at the work of computer department staff. The staff may include systems analysts and programmers, though smaller firms buy the services of such people rather than keeping a team on the payroll. These people's jobs are rather different, so there are separate sections on them.

You are probably working through this book because you hope to get a job in the computing industry. The point of this chapter is not just for us to explore what that may mean — "people and computers" must also cover the theme of the effects of information technology on society. It is not hard to see many of those effects are good — but there are dangers too, and often individuals suffer as a result of computerisation.

8.1   OFFICE SYSTEMS

What is an office?

Historically, an office involves using the basic features of information technology; that is, it handles information. An office takes in information and puts it out; it also has to store, access and process information (see Figure 8.1).

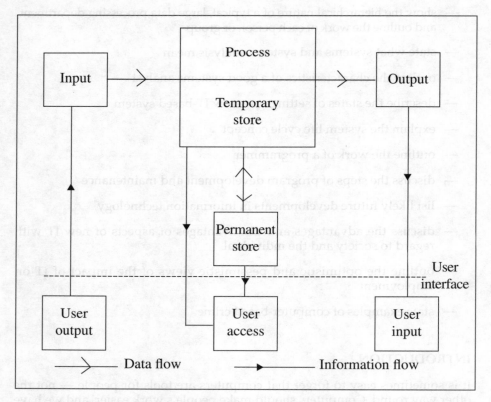

Figure 8.1   An office is an information handling system

Information technology (IT) involves analysing and improving any information handling system. Offices have, of course, evolved over thousands of years; but rapid and huge improvements follow modern IT. This is because the traditional office has depended on information on paper. Paper is bulky, messy, open to loss, abuse and damage, and is very costly, both in itself and with respect to associated working time, equipment and furniture.

IT does not rely on paper, though it links with paper-based systems as need be. Rather, IT is electronic; it offers an office the chance to input, output, process, store and access information electronically all the time. This leads to great savings in costs of all kinds, including those that relate to storage space, security and the time spent on individual tasks. Also, done properly, there are fewer chances of mistakes.

These points are crucial in many cases: some firms deal with such vast amounts of information that without IT to help they could not cope. Examples are government departments, insurance and finance houses, even many scientific research centres. Of course, many of these organisations need good electronic communications as much as good computers: they transfer vast amounts of data daily between their offices, even across the world.

Compared with games or robot control programs, for instance, office software directly concerns handling information in its own right. We have already seen some of the programs in question — word processing, data base management, communications software, the spreadsheet, and graphics in particular.

Figure 8.2 shows all the flows between the functional areas of a firm. Apart from the factory itself (the production sections) and the warehouse, all the departments shown — personnel, accounts, purchasing, sales, goods in, and goods out — are offices as we think of them. Of course, in a small firm, one person may carry all these roles.

The firm's actual function is to obtain raw materials and process them into finished goods; the goods then pass out to the customers. These movements are the firm's various flows of materials. However, you can see that, in order to support that movement of physical items, there are far more flows of information; these are flows of paper in the traditional office. In the modern office, on the other hand, each such flow can be an electronic data transfer; that offers many advantages for fast, efficient and cost effective working. Can you relate each data flow to the use of a particular type of office software?

The information flows include three cash flows: payments to suppliers, payments from customers, and wages and salaries to staff. As far as office working is concerned, and indeed that of the economy as a whole, money is information. Because of this, financial movements are open to handling by information technology just as much as the other types of information transfer in the diagram. Clearly, that is the case in banks and other such firms.

What Figure 8.2 does *not* show is a computing department in the firm in question. (In practice, it may have the name data processing — dp for short.) Many firms have no special department for looking after IT and computing,

though perhaps a senior manager has the task of making sure that systems
develop and are used effectively and compatibly. On the other hand, many
firms have a large dp department, under the leadership of a dp manager.
That department would be responsible for all the electronic information and
money flows. The dp manager would work closely with the other
departments, to ensure that the firm's use of IT meets the firm's needs.

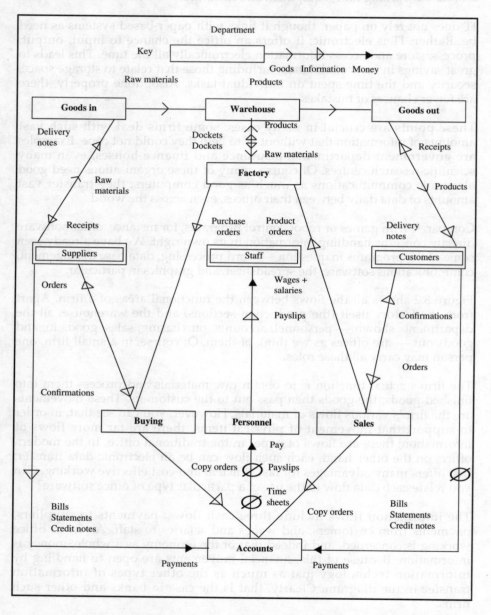

**Figure 8.2 There is a pattern to how information and goods
move round a company**

You already know that such a department will have hardware and software, i.e. equipment and the programs to control it. Some people also talk of the department's "liveware"; that means the staff who work in it and keep everything running smoothly. Let us turn to that now.

8.2 LIVEWARE

A micro, and even a small network, may have no specialist staff to look after it, other than the users themselves; a technician or engineer may drop by every so often. A mainframe, on the other hand, can give employment to a large number of people. It may help to think of these people in two groups — users and others; however, the structure of a typical computing department in a big firm is as shown, hierarchically, in Figure 8.3.

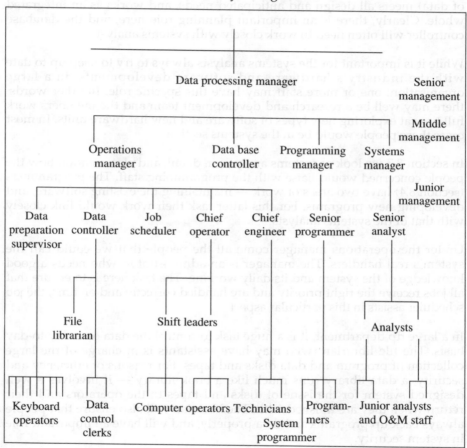

Figure 8.3 A large computer system provides work for many people

The usual name for this part of a firm is the data processing department. Data processing (dp) has long been the name for the handling of business information — its input, storage, processing, transfer and output. When modern IT came to assist, the term electronic data processing (edp) appeared. Now, though, people assume dp involves IT.

The dp manager not only looks after the whole department, but is part of the firm's senior or middle manaement team. Management expertise, is crucial, so too is IT knowledge — thus many dp managers have a systems analysis background (we will come back to that in a while).

Below the dp manager come the people responsible for operations, database control, systems, and programming. They look after their section of the department's work on a day-to-day basis, and consult as required with the others and with the dp manager on short term needs and long term planning.

The database controller is a type of systems analyst (and in a smaller department may work in that section rather than separately). It is this person's task to ensure that at all times the database (the firm's structured set of data) meets all design and anticipated needs, and works as an integrated whole. Clearly, there is an important planning role here, and the database controller will often need to work closely with systems analysts.

While it is important for the systems analysts always to try to keep up to date with the industry's hardware and software developments, in a large organisation, one or more staff may have this specific role. In other words, there may well be a research and development team and the members work full time at exploring new types of software and new hardware units. In most cases these people would be in the systems section.

In section 8.3 we look at systems analysis in detail, and also mention how the people concerned would liaise with the programming staff. The programmers (section 8.4) have two areas of work — maintaining the existing software, and developing new programs. For this latter task their work would link closely with that of the systems analysts.

Under the operations manager come all the people that we could call the system's real handlers. The manager is an administrator, who needs a good knowledge of the system and its daily working. The task here is to ensure that all jobs receive the right priority and are handled correctly and on time, the job scheduler assists in this particular aspect.

In a large dp department, it is a huge task to control the data on a day-to-day basis. The file librarian (who may have assistants is in charge of the large collection of program and data disks and tapes. For reasons of efficiency and security, a data library runs much like a book library — it involves a well designed system for the issue of disks and tapes to the operators and their return when they are finished with. The librarian will also ensure that people always back up programs and data properly, and will have an important role in system security.

The operations staff are the only people who have much contact with the computer itself. Working in the computer room, to which few other people will have access, it is their job to keep the system running smoothly and to provide the peripherals with their needs from moment to moment. There will thus be people whose job is simply to ensure the right disks and tapes are in the right drives at the right times, while others feed paper to the printers, put in new ribbons, and so on.

A large computer department, with hardware worth more than a few million dollars, must work 24 hours a day. This is to make it cost-effective. It is normal, therefore, for there to be three shifts of operating staff; the shift leader of each group will sit at the main console and communicate with the computer. This person has to give the system its instructions, and to react to messages from the processor about completed jobs and problems that arise.

All the work of the dp department depends on the transactions entered each day by the data preparation staff; they are a big section of the real users. A large firm may have hundreds of people entering data each day, either in the same building as the computer, or scattered round the country. These are keyboard operators whose work involves getting data into the system from source documents (like forms, invoices, and questionnaires) and telephone calls.

Clearly, it would not be efficient for the central processor to look after the needs of so many input units; if it does it may have little time left for real processing. Thus, it is normal for the keyboard operators to work off-line using a separate key to store (eg key to disk) approach. This involves a separate computer, maybe a mini, which works full time on collating the input data into one or more transaction files. A major task of the night shift staff will be to merge the previous day's transaction files with the master files, and produce new masters for the next day.

There are, of course, other computing users within a firm — secretarial staff and typists using word processors, people working with accounts software and other business programs, and all the staff searching for information. Many of these people may well use standalone micros or one or more networks not linked full time to the main computer.

The dp manager will have responsibility for all IT equipment used within the firm; however, apart from dealing with problems and providing advice, the dp staff will have little day-to-day contact with these other users.

The same may well apply to the firm's systems analysis staff. Their role is to design the firm's hardware/software package (system), and the ways of using it, and then to ensure it keeps up-to-date with needs. That is a very different kind of task from that of the other people mentioned here. In fact only the largest firms have their own permanent staff for this kind of work. Probably most systems analysts work as consultants, bought in when needed.

8.3 SYSTEMS ANALYSIS

Many people in the computing and IT industries think systems analysts have the most exciting and rewarding lives. Certainly a really good one can have an excellent career and be very well paid indeed for the trouble. All the same, systems analysis requires a lot of training and experience, very hard work and very hard thinking.

The job involves first looking with great care at the needs of an organisation (eg a firm), and at how they are meeting those needs at the moment (if, indeed, they are). The next step is to decide if the current system for dealing with those needs is the best one. Here, the word system does *not* mean a computer system (a complete set of hardware, software and liveware used to carry out a task). The word is more general: the complete set of people, procedures, and aids used to carry out the task which may include a computer system. It is this kind of system a systems analyst analyses.

Having analysed the firm's needs and its current system, and decided the latter is not the best way to meet the former, the analyst tries to design a more suitable system. Again, note this need *not* be an IT-based one; normally, though, it is — because many of a firm's tasks concern information handling. In any event, the aim is to work out how to meet the firm's present and likely future needs most effectively.

Lastly, it is likely the systems analyst will watch over the introduction of the new system (that is, if the firm agrees to go ahead). After that there may be an on-going remote supervision role.

As we have seen, most big firms have a systems analyst or two of their own; indeed some have large systems analysis departments. The latter may include more junior organisation and methods (O&M) staff as well as graduate analysts. A small firm, on the other hand, will call in this kind of expertise from outside when needed. As a result, many systems analysts and some O&M people are consultants — working on their own or as partners in a specialist group. Also, many computer bureaux can supply systems analysis expertise. (A specialist firm that rents out computer time, staff and expertise. It may well also run training courses using its own specialist staff.)

In any case, the people concerned need a deep, wide and always up-to-date knowledge and experience of IT in the widest sense.

In a given contract, the systems analyst is likely to work through all or most of these stages:

— defining the problem in outline and then in depth

— carrying out a feasibility study

— fact finding

— systems analysis itself

— new systems design

— new systems implementation

— systems maintenance.

People call this set of stages a system's life cycle. The name implies a circular process. This is as it should be — circumstances change (inside a firm, in its areas of interest, and in IT), so any system needs constant review.

Having defined what is to be done, the analyst carries out a feasibility study. This means getting enough information about the client to decide whether full study and analysis are likely to be worthwhile. It may well be that, for the time being, the current system is close enough to the best to make any change a matter of pointless expense and upset.

Fact finding is most important. This is carrying out a highly detailed review of the work being done at the moment and the system (methods) involved. The analyst's golden rule is to know clearly the context of the problem being looked at. The philosophy of fact finding includes:

— finding out the hierarchical structure of the client firm and methods of working within it

— having an open mind at all times (people's views of their work may not be correct)

— being flexible in the methods used (no two firms are the same)

— finding out who the experts are (they may, in fact, be low down on the ladder)

— being prepared to rely on hunches to some extent (having a feel for one's work is of great value).

The main methods used in the fact finding stage are:

— collecting relevant papers

— interviewing staff, and maybe some of the firm's clients

— quiet observation

—questionnaires.

The work cannot be rushed; fact finding for a major project may take several analysts a couple of years. This is why large firms have their own full-time analysts — they constantly study what is going on and how it may be improved.

Quite often, a new system is needed for some procedure that does not yet exist. For instance, a chain of shops may wish to extend to mail order. In this case the analyst will work mainly with the people who are planning the change and try to find out what they want to achieve. Even so, a great deal of the above kind of fact finding is needed.

Once the hundreds or thousands of facts have been collected and sorted out the next step is to analyse the problem and the system and produce a summary report. Often the analyst may set this out in the form of a flowchart, a picture tends to be easier to study and work with than a lot of text; and it is often much more compact. The report shows the information flows into, through, and out of the system, rather like Figure 8.2. (As in other contexts, information may well include money). The report outlines, too, the analyst's proposals for change (if any), and gives some idea of cost and timescale.

The analyst's report usually goes to the firm's management for consideration. It is they who must decide whether they agree with the content and whether they wish (and can afford) to go ahead with the outlined proposals.

Once the client has agreed to proceed, the analyst will define and design the new system — the processes to do the job. Now is the stage at which the analyst looks at different ways of meeting the needs found, and it is at this stage that comparison of the various solutions that involve IT are made, as well as those that don't. (If the best solution found does not involve IT — which is not rare — then the rest of the analyst's work on that contract is not relevant here).

This stage of systems analysis involves working out the best solution. How exactly can new information technology help? What are the precise computing needs? How should the hardware link into a local network or with systems elsewhere? What programs will carry out the tasks involved? How much can the IT systems that the client already has be used?

If there is software on the market that can do the needed work, this will help determine what central processor should be bought in. That is because as yet no software runs on all computers; the current big problem of incompatibility, while getting smaller, will remain into the next century.

If no current software fits the user's needs, the analyst will call on a programmer to tailor something to suit, or even invite a programming team to produce a software suite from scratch. A big firm with its own systems analysts will likely have this expertise on tap too. Even if that is the case, the analyst will need to gain management approval at this stage; software development can cost more than hardware purchase.

The analyst will devise a broad chart for the programmers, with notes on the files to be used (nature, content, type, structure), and on input and output data types and hardware. When those concerned have agreed the details, the programmers can get on with the job. See section 8.4.

In designing the hardware/software system, the analyst always keeps in mind the following questions:

— Who are the users — and therefore how simple can we make the system?

— How easy is it to obtain the information needed to feed the system?

— How many different tasks can we carry out without making the system too complex?

While all this time the analyst will have kept management informed of progress, when the hardware has been chosen it is time to get full approval to go ahead with purchase (or rental) and installation. The analyst must be able to provide detailed costings, to write good, clear, short reports, and to discuss these fully with non-experts as well as with experts.

Once the hardware and software are approved, the analyst schedules introduction. This needs close work with all the people concerned with usage — that includes the cleaning, security and catering staff as well as, perhaps, architects, builders, designers, and suppliers.

At the same time the analyst will start to prepare detailed documentation for the actual users. Again, it is crucial to be able to communicate effectively, this time, not just with management and other professionals.

It is also the analyst's responsibility to prepare detailed test data and plans to check out the completed system, and to arrange the tests. Once this is done it is time to prepare a final schedule to put the new system into full operation, and to assist the users to prepare for it.

During the actual implementation of the new computer system, the analyst will have to deal at once with anything that goes wrong. This is not easy, as there will be a stage of parallel running — with the old system still in use while people check and then test the new one with real data. The analyst may well have a training role at this time too.

That may all make it sound as if systems analysts are super-human. Don't forget that in practice a team, perhaps a large one, will handle a big project, and will work closely with management. Also O&M staff may help with the less demanding parts of the work. All the same, an analyst must be:

— an expert in hardware, software, management and finance

— highly literate and able with numbers

— imaginative

— a good listener and communicator

— a good seller of ideas

— patient and tactful

— very attentive to detail.

The work of systems analysts is important in all stages of the so-called system life cycle. That phrase describes the development and implementation of a new system for carrying out a task or set of tasks. It also implies, by using the word "cycle", that development and implementation never finish, that the systems analyst's job is rather like cleaning the town's streets: when you get to the end, you have to start again.

The table below links the stages of the system life cycle with the skills a systems analyst needs. Check to see that it makes sense.

Life cycle stage	Systems analyst's skills
Use current system	Observation
Recognise (potential) problem(s)	Management
Define problem	Precision
Carry out feasibility study (including fact finding)	Thoroughness, tact
Report	Literacy, marketing, management
Design new system	IT, imagination, thoroughness
Implement new system	IT, market knowledge
Document new system	Precision, literacy
Test new system	Programming, thoroughness, imagination
Supervise training	Management, tact
Supervise parallel running	Management, thoroughness, tact

Life cycle stage	Systems analyst's skills cont'd
Phase out old system	Management, tact
Maintain system	IT
Back to start	Patience

8.4   THE PROGRAMMER AT WORK

Like the systems analyst, the programmer is not closely involved in the day-to-day work of the data processing department. Again, in a large firm the department may employ a number of such people (but they will not have close contact with the others). On the other hand, a small firm (or its systems analyst) will take on programming staff just for a particular job.

Programming involves the design of an ordered set of instructions, in a form the computer can follow, to carry out some given task. Crucial concepts in program development — *not* the same as programming (coding) itself — are planning, developing the idea in stages from the top down, aiming for software that is efficient and friendly.

Efficiency in programming means having a product which:

— works as you plan in all contexts

— works at the right speed

— uses as little memory as possible

— looks good to all who see it.

The essence of program design is an approach called top-down development. This means breaking your initial idea into smaller and more detailed chunks — concepts — until at last each one is a unit that is easy to handle. In practice we use the words module for each of those final units. The sketch in Figure 8.4 shows what the planning part of top-down programming entails; the original broad concept fragments into a lot of small chunks, mind-sized ones for easy brain-storming.

The picture is a hierarchical one, a bit like the structure of our lungs — and for much the same reason — efficiency of processing.

Coding itself—turning the idea into a full working program — is a lengthy process that requires a lot of care. The final main stage is testing the product. Here are the questions to ask:

— Does the program carry out its design task?

— Does it do so efficiently, quickly, and (in the case of numerical work) to the correct levels of accuracy?

— Does it handle all conceivable cases?

— Can it cope with all conceivable inputs?

Testing is therefore much more than just seeing if the program runs and gives results. Indeed, it is as important to plan your testing process as to plan the program itself. You need to seek out and destroy various kinds of error (bug).

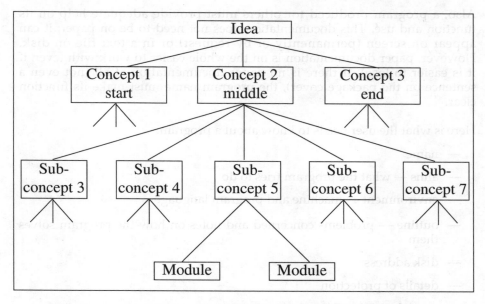

Figure 8.4 Top-down planning—the essence of programming

Aiming for user-friendliness (a good user interface) is also a crucial part of software design. As well as working correctly and efficiently, the program must appeal to the user in other ways: that person should always be at ease and never wonder what to do. (This is mainly, but not only for interactive programs).

The most important thing here concerns planning the screen layout and the messages on it. Each message should be short but clear, well laid out and not cramped (and properly spelled and punctuated). For example:

— a minimum of capital letters

— highlighting methods such as inverse, italic, special symbols, under-lining and framing — but not too much

— colour — the same applies

— sound — the same applies

— time delays to help break down a page

— blank lines between paragraphs

— full or partial screen clearing to erase old messages.

Such techniques greatly help the user — unless you overdo them. It is very poor practice to have fairly simple text in a dozen colours, half of them flashing crudely at you, and silly tunes playing at the same time.

The best way to test the user interface is to try the program out on other (honest) people, and to carefully watch their reactions.

Also, a program produced for others must provide adequate help on its function and use. This documentation does not need to be on paper; it can appear on screen (permanently or by request) or in a text file on disk. However, paper documentation is on the whole easier to work with (even if it is easier to lose). If there is no paper documentation at all (not even a sentence on the package cover), the program name must make its function clear.

Here is what the user needs to know about a program:

— name

— aims — what the program tries to do

— environment — machine and program language

— outline — problems concerned and notes on how the program solves them

— disk address

— details of protection

— special peripheral requirements

— author name(s)

— date

— source (where the idea came from in the first place) and other acknowledgements

— loading details

— input formats accepted (if not clear from screen messages)

— unacceptable inputs and other limitations

— outputs to be expected

— ideas and instructions for the various uses

— relevant references.

User documentation must include as little technical language as possible. There can be shortcuts and technical sections for the "experts", however, and final package testing should include letting others work with the draft documentation as well as with the software.

After the software is truly finished, the work of programmers is not at an end. There may, of course, be new programs to write, but even if that is not the case, there is a major role in software maintenance.

What is software maintenance? — in essence it consists of:

— adding new procedures and removing old ones as the firm's needs change

— linking programs together in new ways for the same reason

— dealing with bugs as people find these

— increasing the efficiency of the programs

— enabling the software to work with new peripherals

— perhaps some role in system security.

In other words, the programmer has the job of keeping the software up-to-date; it must always be able to change to meet the changing needs of the firm. Programmers must bear that future aim in mind as they work on a new package — each program must be easy to amend, and there must be full documentation on paper to explain how that may be done.

8.5 INFORMATION TECHNOLOGY

Where is information technology (IT) taking us?

IT's concern is the storage, access, processing and transferring of information quickly and cheaply, and in a way from which all concerned can gain the most.

In the global village future, all people have cheap, effective access to the information they need and want. Various scenarios could let that happen; all depend on worldwide availability of the right hardware, the right software, and a cheap means of high volume information storage and transfer. Cable and satellite links can provide this, and progress in hardware will continue its amazing pace. As far as storage is concerned, floppy magnetic disks are moving to capacities ten times higher than now; hard disks, digital audio tape (dat), compact and video disks will show an increase in storage space of the same order. Within a decade, computer users could have as much information locally on line as they may wish.

Continued miniaturisation with its spin-off of increased reliability and reduced costs is significant too. (This is so in such areas as electric motors — some now fit on to the chips that carry their control circuits, and are a tenth of a millimetre across). Super-conductivity may reduce to nearly zero the electric power demands of hardware units and network links, while bio-electronics brings people and machines much closer together.

With regard to programs, we can expect highly integrated software in artificially intelligent systems, plus multiprocessing, the ability to handle large quantities of data at speed using a number of programs in a number of processors at the same time.

While most of these developments will first affect large organisations, they will rapidly spread to the small firm, to education and training, and to the home.

Thus, a scenario near one of the spectrum sees a global satellite and cable network linking each work, living and leisure unit. In the unit — office, school, shop, home, cafe — is an adequate supply of intelligent workstations. Current progress in machine intelligence and true concurrent processing could lead to those coming to be spread through the building, as shown in Figure 8.5.

Talking with a computer tucked away out of sight may give people problems. Anyway, it may not always be the best way to get information into and out of a computer: think of noise and security problems.

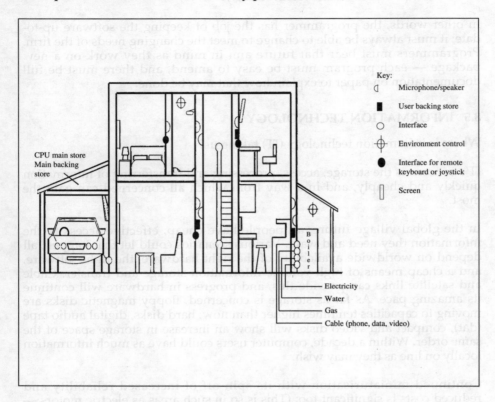

CPU main store
Main backing
store

Key:

◖ Microphone/speaker

■ User backing store

○ Interface

⊕ Environment control

● Interface for remote keyboard or joystick

▯ Screen

Boiler

— Electricity
— Water
— Gas
— Cable (phone, data, video)

Figure 8.5   The home computer of 2001

Perhaps then there will always be a need for visual displays, for instance to let you study tables of information, views of products or places, and data in text, table or graphic form. The large flat wall unit will show:

— broadcast and recorded tv

— the face of the person across the world with whom you are holding a telephone call

— frames from any of many videotex databases (teletext and viewdata)

— documents and pictures from microform and video disk archives

— restful scenes from your library of pet landscape photos

— computer generated graphics to match your mood by a kind of living wallpaper.

The software driving the display would of course offer windows (a split screen feature in other words) in all these contexts, so you could keep an eye on, or work with, information from various sources at once. The cable system has a lot to carry...

Near the other end of the scale is a world in which each unit is fairly self-sufficient in information There would be much the same hardware but in most cases users would work with information on the unit's own bank of chips and disks. The social view behind this particular world involves the idea of the village in a true sense — one where people relate to each other in a tight local community rather than round the globe as a whole.

Current thinking seems to lean towards a unification of world communications, and thus some easing in their use, rather than a fragmentation. But can IT really reduce the stresses that seem to come with the current style of living and working?

One way that could reduce those stresses at work is a much increased degree of telecommuting. In this view, the need for local and long distance business travel falls as information transfer — communication — becomes faster and cheaper. In the case of many jobs, working from home or from a base down the street is no problem if there is a global cable network. The videophone and its potential for video-conferences should reduce the urge for face to face meetings. Better expert systems, universal and fast electronic mail, interactive video, electronic and desktop publishing, fax and better versions of most things we have looked at should all reduce the need for travel.

There are many possible IT-based views of the future. Hardware, software, machine intelligence and telecommunications links will all continue to improve, cheapen and spread — whatever the social system. What happens depends on how people decide to use what is on offer rather than on changed technology. Choice therefore is concerned with how to give all the people concerned a fuller life — less drudgery, less boredom, more freedom to do their own thing in their own way. This should be the case wherever we end up on that spectrum of IT futures.

Living with IT should not mean just coping with the technology, but using it as a positive aid to dealing with our needs in society.

8.6 COMPUTERS AND SOCIETY

Systems analysts have often noted that their clients are afraid of the new system. Without doubt, it is a fact that many people, well educated or not, show real fear or express concern about the current "information revolution". On the other hand, many welcome new information technology; they do so on the grounds that it can extend and free the power of the human brain — in the same way as the "industrial revolution" produced machines to extend and free the power of human muscle.

It is not hard to take that comparison further. If you do so you may think of people's fears and society's problems when the major industrial revolution got under way in 18th century Britain. The times were marked by much concern about machines taking work from humans — just as now so many people worry about loss of employment as a result of computers and robots.

It is crucial to realise that one's point of view makes a lot of difference. If IT helps a firm become more efficient, this may be a good thing for a large, number of people, both in the firm and outside it. That will be the case even if the number of staff employed falls; there is a lot of commonsense in taking productivity — output per person — as a measure of efficiency. All the same, the staff members who lose their jobs as a direct result of IT won't feel quite the same about it.

Properly applied, IT has without doubt the power to make many kinds of organisations more efficient, and thus to improve society as a whole. Most of us would agree that an improved society is one whose members:

— lead longer and more pleasant lives

— have more money and more goods

— have more leisure

— face less hassle, less pain, less drudgery.

However, as society improves, it should not do so by the careless sacrifice of individuals. It is important for progress to be humane.

Humane progress is more likely if the members of society are aware of what is going on, otherwise there are those who may exploit another person's lack of awareness. There is a belief that a society whose individuals can discuss the nature of life and its trends, and who can come to terms with (even if not affect) change, is better than one where this is not the case. Information technology has done much in its own public relations cause, but it is a pity that people involved in different aspects of its work find it hard to explain to others what they are doing. Computer jargon is a real barrier to the communications and discussions we need.

The basic argument is for the introduction or extension of IT in society, even at the cost of jobs. Without IT the firms and organisations concerned (included in this are individuals and their homes) would become less efficient. In such cases they would become less able to survive. In other words, there may be even greater job losses and even more misery if firms and people do not computerise and automate.

The argument then goes on, in that an organisation using IT can grow as a result of the increase in demand for cheaper goods and services that follows improved efficiency. It can then employ more staff, have them work shorter hours, pay them more, and still provide more goods more cheaply to the rest of society.

Lastly, as the firms, their staff and their customers pay more tax as a result of the above, society will be better able to support its dependants — the unemployed, the young, the retired and the sick.

There are two sides to many other related arguments. For instance, some people feel that for workers to have computers or robots to help would reduce morale, because they would have less responsibility. On the other hand, there are those who say that having such help will give people more freedom (in other words, more time and energy) for more interesting tasks, in particular for planning. While there is some truth in the latter view, people are expected to be fairly well educated, and also to have a positive attitude to change. This may involve more re-training, for instance. Indeed, by the next century, some people may find themselves re-trained three or four times during their working lives.

Most of the comments made so far in this section applied just as much to the "industrial revolution" as they apply to the present spread of information technology. The most important social effect of the former was not the feared fall in employment (indeed the opposite happened) it was the major change in the structure of society that followed.

Within a few decades, Britain changed from a society whose population lived and worked on the land, to an industrial system with most of the people living in towns and working in offices and factories. Will the present "revolution" have any such sweeping effect on society as a whole?

This question is just as significant as that of employment. Again, there is little to say about it, except to give just a few pointers to thought and talk.

Claiming that we are seeing a major shift from employment in industry to employment in information related work and the service industries is a bit too simple. In particular, it may make you feel society is turning into a society of parasites, one whose members do not truly contribute. It is also easy to infer from that statement that production will fall, and therefore that society will become poorer. This is not the case.

Britain became extremely rich in the 19th century because machines helped people to create wealth. It is now possible for society to gain further wealth by letting computers and robots help people. Indeed, this was mentioned when we looked at the effects of IT on employment. In the same way the industrial revolution led to farms, ships, mines, and factories (and very many other organisations) being able to run with greater efficiency with only a handful of people.

In this chapter we have already looked at a possible future in which a first-world country like Britain has reached social equilibrium following the upheaval of the information revolution, and is one which every home, workplace, and public area links to an IT network (the cable system) making information very cheap, easy to access, and easy to share. It also raised the concept of telecommuting in which very many people work from home, using IT links as needed.

Should telecommuting become the norm — as some people think it could — a major reason for the existence of towns and cities would vanish: the main modern function of towns and cities would be as work centres with residential suburbs.

Perhaps, then, the information revolution might reverse the result of the industrial revolution, and return the population to a much more even spread over the land. This may remove urban problems — heavy traffic, noise, dirt, the troubles of the inner cities. On the other hand, it could also lead to a fragmentation of society that not all would welcome.

Again, there are opposing points of view. Some people fear the home is becoming an IT cocoon from which most people would never venture; others note the tremendous growth in leisure pursuits in recent decades and expect that to continue.

Perhaps there is little any one person can do about any of the trends discussed here. However, being aware of what is going on is what matters. So too is being prepared to form reasoned views of what life should be like; to make them public and even to campaign for them. Also, other causes for concern about which more can be done. These include computer-related crime and IT abuse in a concrete sense. In this context, security concerns setting up safeguards to protect data (in the widest sense) from being copied, erased, or changed with criminal intent.

Strictly we should define computer crime as criminal acts which could not happen without computers. People often blame IT for many crimes which have long existed just because the criminals now use computers to help them.

Currently, computer criminals in the strictest sense tend to be clever, fairly young, professional people who at least start with the simple aim of beating a security system — meeting a challenge in other words. They then take unfair advantage of the system once they have cracked the security system.

The security system in question may be in their own place of work or elsewhere; if the former is the case there may also be a feeling of getting revenge for some real or imagined insult or lack of promotion. The challenge aspect of computer crime is enforced by the fairly common practice of not taking such a criminal to court once caught; this seems to be on the grounds that the publicity could cause loss of confidence in the firm concerned once found out. Indeed, quite a few of these poachers turn gamekeeper by taking up work in computer security.

There are two main classes of computer crime. The first involves theft of electronic money; the second is theft of electronic information. In either case, the approach would be to divert the money or the information from where it should be to where the criminal can access it. Moving a cent from each of a bank's account to the criminal's own account, and hacking into a supposedly secure database are examples of these two classes.

Keeping a system — hardware, software and database — secure involves trying to set up methods by which only authorised people can access it; it is also providing checks to detect and prevent abuse. Allowing only a few people to enter the computer area, providing it with a separate power supply; setting up multi-layer levels of passwords (especially for remote users), and ensuring no one person has access to too large a section — all these are methods of improving security. However, no computer system can be totally

secure from abuse, especially abuse by someone who knows it well.
Firms whose computers store highly sensitive information will also try to
ensure they fully check in advance all who have access. They will then issue
them with electronic key-cards so they can enter only certain rooms, and
special keys to switch on their terminals, as well as providing them with
passwords.

Part of the function of the operating software will be to keep a record of who
logs on, when, at what terminal, and for how long, as well as the software
and/or data they access. There will be security guards in and around the
building, and certain staff will have, at all times, the right to look at what
each member of staff is doing. Data printed out on paper goes to a shredder
rather than just being thrown away when it is no longer needed, and highly
complex programs code data before transfer to a remote terminal.

All these methods are costly; indeed in some organisations security may now
come near the top of the budget of running costs. Even so, no system is
perfect. The computer industry is after all a young one; it may be some
decades before we can feel that electronic data is truly safe.

It is particularly important, in a free society, to protect data about individuals.
The use of computers to store and process personal data has grown rapidly.
Thus, it is very likely that details about *you* are to be found in various
computers around the country; it is important to try to keep what is held
secure from abuse. Doing this involves keeping data private.

Abuse is applying the stored data for a purpose it is not designed for; in
particular to damage the rights of the individuals concerned. Blackmail comes
to mind; so too does making up mailing lists for junk letters, and building up
profiles of householders so sales staff can approach them with highly
personalised offers.

As a result, many countries have set up data protection laws in an attempt to
protect personal data. If yours does not — should it?

In Britain, data users must follow a code of practice, and ensure their staff
follow the rules. They must:

— collect and process personal data fairly and lawfully

— hold personal data only for registered lawful purposes

— disclose data only to registered recipients and approved countries

— ensure that data held is adequate, relevant, accurate and up-to-date

— delete personal data when it is no longer needed

— use appropriate security measures

— allow data subjects to have access.

The first of these principles means that data obtained by deceit is not lawful.
It is therefore against the law to collect personal data if you pretend to carry

out a market survey when your true intentions are different, for instance. The other aims are more obvious — and they all have the task of protecting each of us from computer-related abuse.

NOW TRY THESE...

1. Try as many different keyboards as you can. Compare them on the grounds of ease of use, comfort, efficiency and cost.

2. Will we ever have a cashless society?

3. Discuss briefly some of the developments in computing that have led to the widespread use of computers in homes, offices and factories.

4. What is automation? If it contributes to lower employment, is it a good thing?

5. Would you like to telecommute?

6. Would you like to live in an IT-based "global village"?

7. How much could the IT-based home of 2001 affect formal schooling? In what other ways may IT affect formal schooling? What barriers may make the changes to formal schooling come about more slowly than they could?

Appendix 1
Glossary

Here are brief notes on the main technical terms used in the book. The entries are for initial reference only—this is not an encyclopedia. However, the material should provide enough information to help you in your reading and to understand more detailed explanation elsewhere. Please also refer to the index and, in general, to the IT dictionary or glossary you have to hand. An excellent reference is *A Dictionary of Information Technology and Computer Science*, 2nd Edition, by Tony Gunton (NCC Blackwell, 1993).

Access	Getting back information from a store—eg a chip, a disk or a tape.
Address	Number, label or code that identifies a particular cell in a computer store or a sector on a disk, there being various styles of addressing.
AI	Machine (artificial) intelligence.
Algol	The first structured high-level program language (1962), which led to Pascal.
Algorithm	The solution to a problem in the form of a logical series of steps.
ALU	Arithmetic and logic unit.
Analog(ue)	A real world measure (eg time, acidity, pressure, weight) that varies smoothly in value rather than being stepped (digital).
Analysis	Working out the structure and action of a system in terms of its parts, the aim perhaps being to make the structure simpler and the action more efficient.
Applications software	Program that applies a computer to a real world problem, eg handling accounts or driving a robot.
Applications program generator (APG)	A fourth generation language system that allows a user to define the broad details of a program (eg input/output and files) and then outputs the program code for the task.

Architecture	The logical (effective) layout of a circuit, device, system or network.
Arithmetic ant logic unit (ALU)	Where a processor carries out (binary) arithmetic processes and logical comparisons.
Artificial intelligence	Machine intelligence.
Assembly language	A low level program language that uses coded versions of English words to give instructions to a processor, plus labels to refer to data items and addresses. An assembler program automatically translates these into machine code.
Asynchronous	Data transfer which takes place when the data is ready, rather than when a pulse from outside tells it to.
Backing store	Large scale external memory, based on tape or disk, for instance, that supports a system's main store.
Barrel printer	A type of line printer whose characters lie over the surface of a fast turning drum.
Basic	Beginners All-purpose Symbolic Instruction Code — a very common high-level program language, with, however, many dialects.
Batch processing	Non-interactive computing where the computer works in turn through a set (batch) of programs and the data provided in advance for them.
Baud	A rate of data transfer of about a bit per second.
Belt printer	A type of line printer whose characters lie along the length of a fast turning belt or chain.
Binary number	A number that consists only of the digits 0 and 1, perhaps with a binary point, the place values being powers of 2: 12 4 8.
Block	The smallest unit in a backing store medium you can address or transfer.
Bubble store	Store made of chips which have a magnetic surface, with moving domains in the surface that can stand for 0s and 1s.
Bug	A mistake in a system or program removed by debugging.

Byte	A group of, typically, eight bits that can stand for any keyboard character or control code.
Cartridge	A compact hardware, firmware or backing storage pack, eg a tape loop in a box.
CCD	Charge coupled device.
CD	Compact disk with CD-I being compact disk interactive and CD-ROM being compact disk read only memory.
Central processing unit (CPU)	The main processing control unit in traditional computer architectures.
Chain printer	A line printer with the characters held on the surface of a chain or belt.
Character	Any number, letter, symbol or control code for a keyboard, screen or printer, in a file.
Character printer	One which in effect prints a character at a time.
Charge coupled device	Basis of a new form of data storage, the bits being held as tiny chunks of electric charge on the surface of the device.
Chief operator	The person in charge of the daily operations of a computer suite.
Chip	A tiny piece of semiconductor that can contain complex electronic circuits.
Cobol	COmmon Business Oriented Language — a high-level program language widely used in business.
Code	To write out a computer program, the chunks of program that result also being code. Codes are also a way to compress data so it takes up less space in a channel or a store.
Communications software	Programs that let you transfer messages and data files over a distance, often using a phone link.
Compact disk (CD)	12 cm disk that can store vast amounts of digital data. This leads to CD-ROM (CD-read only memory), which puts bulk data on-line to a computer in read only form. Another field is CD-I (compact disk interactive); this has an approach rather like that of interactive video.
Compile	To translate, with a compiler, the whole of a high-level language source program into a machine code object program.

Computer	A modern high-speed stored program digital electronic data processor.
Console	which a system's chief operator or shift leader works, to monitor and control the flow of jobs.
Consultant	An expert in some aspect of IT, with no ties to any particular system or supplier, and therefore able to give you valid aid and advice.
Consumables	Anything you need a regular supply of, such as printer paper and fuses.
Continuous stationery	Paper in continuous form, roll, or fan-fold, instead of in separate sheets.
Control	The field of automating and managing processes and machines, including the control of robots.
Control unit	The part of a processor which looks after the operation of the system by controlling the action of the other units on the basis of instructions.
Conversational	Interactive.
Core store	Main store.
CPU	Central processor unit.
Cursor	A symbol on a screen that shows where you are — perhaps a square blob or underline mark, often flashing.
Cycle time	The time taken by a processor to handle a single instruction.
Cylinder	In a disk pack the set of all tracks with the same number, ie all those the head unit can access without moving.
Daisy wheel	The central part in a high quality (but slow) character printer — a wheel without a rim with the characters at the ends of the spokes (petals).
Data	Generally, coded information, ie with no obvious meaning, even if in the form of letters or numbers people can read.
Database	A collection of data organised into a structure on the basis of the relationships between the data items concerned, so as to make processing, searching and sorting easy.

Data control	Looking after the flow of (programs and) data into a large computer system.
Data entry	Keying data into a system, especially into a large database, normally using a key-to-store technique.
Data item	A single unit of data.
Data processing (DP)	Loosely the handling of information, usually referring in practice to the batch processing by computer of large volumes of prepared data, such as gas bills or payslips.
Debug	To remove mistakes (bugs), a debugger being a special program to help clear errors.
Desktop publishing	Software (also called page layout) you can use with a compact in-house computer system to produce pages of well laid out text and graphics ready for printing.
Device	A hardware unit with a single clear function, a device driver being a utility program or routine for working it.
Digital	Anything that can be counted as separate numbers, the opposite of analogue — a digital signal being step-like, while an analogue one is wavy.
Digitiser	Any device able to give a digital output from some form of analogue input.
Disk	A flat circular sheet of material used to store information; it may be hard (rigid) or flexible (floppy). Disks for computer data storage may be magnetic or optical (like compact video disks).
Disk drive	A device that lets you retrieve (read) data from and record (write) to a disk.
Disk pack	A set of hard disks with a single spindle, addressed by cylinder, surface, sector.
Distributed processing	The arrangement of a network which shares processing tasks and data stores between stations.
Documentation	The instructions and manuals needed to get the best from a system.
Dot matrix	A character printer whose output consists of a series of dot patterns formed by pins striking ink from the ribbon onto the paper.

DP	Data processing, as with the DP departments of most large firms, with dp managers in charge.
Drum printer	Barrel printer — in a drum plotter the paper moves back and forth while the pen moves to and fro.
Duplex	Two way — a data channel that can carry signals both ways at once.
Electronic office	An office (information handling centre) where a great deal of IT used.
Electronics	The technology of systems that involve small electric currents.
Encoding	Changing input data into a form the system can handle.
EPROM	Erasable programmable read only memory (store), type of permanent storage chip whose contents you can change.
Ergonomics	The study of the relationship between the design of equipment and systems and the comfort and efficiency of the user(s).
Errors	Bugs in a program which programmers and users must be on the lookout for.
Expert system	Software that builds up expertise in making judgements from input evidence, and thus displays a form of machine intelligence.
Feasibility study	A stage in systems analysis during which one compares possible solutions to needs.
Field	The space for a single data item (attribute, such as age or code number) in each record of a database.
File	A data structure with a single name: a set of instructions (program), text (document), or other data (part of a database) in a computer's main or backing store.
File maintenance	Keeping the data in a file up-to-date and backed up.
Firmware	Intermediate between software and hardware, holding instructions semi-permanently, usually in the form of ROM chips.

Flat bed	A plotter on the flat surface on which the paper is fixed while the pen moves up and down and to and fro over it (compare drum).
Floppy	See disk.
Flowchart	A method of showing an algorithm or the sequence of actions in a system using boxes joined with arrowed lines.
Format	(s) A piece of text — its layout, headings, spacing and margins (b) Data — its arrangement in a file, on a disk, or on a screen (c) To format a disk and prepare it to receive information in the form suited to your system.
Fortran	Formula Translator — a high-level program language for use in science, etc.
Full duplex	Two way data channel that can carry signals both ways at once.
Function key	Keyboard whose action the user or software defines rather than being fixed.
Generations	Classification of IT systems by type of electronics used by age: (a) first generation: using valves (b) second generation: using transistors (c) third generation: using chips (d) fourth generation: using very complex chips
Graphics	Pictures you can guide a processor to draw on screen or print onto paper.
Graphics pad	A form of digitiser; an input device on which you trace a shape that appears on screen and is coded in digital form for the computer to process, store and output.
Hard disk	A high speed, high density backing storage medium that can hold much more infomation than a floppy, but is often fixed in the computer.
Hardware	The equipment that makes up an IT system, as opposed to the software that drives it.
Header	Set of data at the start of a file, giving basic information such as name, type and length.

High-level (program language A language like Basic or Cobol, in which instructions use English-like words, labels and advanced structures, for translation by compiler or interpreter into machine code, and in which programming relates to problems rather than to machine level activities.

High resolution graphics Computer-generated pictures with a lot of detail which can, for instance, show smooth curves.

Hypertext A form of three-dimensional word processor that allows links between words and phrases, and perhaps graphics, in the various levels.

Implementation Carrying out a program idea or a system design.

Index A list of key field ranges and addresses on a disk that gives direct access to the records of an indexed or indexed sequential file.

Information Information adding to human knowledge, data with meaning (or, to some, structure).

Information technology (IT) Modern methods of collecting, handling, storing and passing information, as text, graphics or sound. The UNESCO definition is: the scientific, technological and engineering disciplines and the management techniques used in information handling and processing; their applications; computers and their interaction with people and machines, and associated social, economic and cultural matters.

Inkjet The design of a compact, fast, quiet printer which sprays tiny drops of ink onto the paper.

Input To feed data into a system (also a noun meaning what is fed in), with an input device (eg sensor or keyboard) having the function of aiding this.

Integrated circuit (IC) Chip.

Integrated software Programs designed as a suite so you can feed data from one automatically into a second intelligent smart peripheral (eg terminal) with its own processing power and store.

Interactive Two way communication— what one side does depends on the response just received from the other, and vice versa. Interactive (conversational) computing is the opposite of batch processing.

Interface	The join between two devices — to interface, to transfer data.
Interpreter	A translating program that translates and carries out high-level language program instructions only when it comes to them, rather than changing a program as a whole into machine code (as does a compiler).
Interrupt	A signal telling the processor to stop what it is doing and handle other work.
IT	Information technology.
JCL	Job control language (see job).
Job	A single program task, especially in a batch processing system where job control language (JCL) programs are how the operator or programmer gives the system commands.
Joystick	A computer input device with a short lever which moves freely in any direction, often used in place of a keyboard with computer software, and also called a paddle.
Key	A field through which you search a file or database for specific records.
Kimball tag	Small punched card on an item of clothing that carries details in machine readable form.
LAN	Local area network.
Laser printer	A fast quality page printer.
Library	The set of disks or tapes used by a dp section (the responsibility of the data librarian) or programs and sub-programs used by a programmer.
Light pen	A pointing device with a photo-cell in the head, with which you can select from choices on a screen, or (sometimes) draw shapes directly on to
Line printer	A printer that in effect constructs a line of output at a time.
Linker	Utility that joins two or more separate machine code programs into one.

Liveware	Jargon for the people running a computer system.
Load	To copy data from backing store into main store. A loader is a utilty that puts into main store a machine code program ready to run.
Local area network (LAN)	A method of linking a set of nearby computers and peripherals.
Log	A continuous timed record of what is happening, eg a computer log is a printout from the operating software of jobs done, problems met, access tried, and actions taken.
Loop network	A network which links the machines in the form of a closed ring.
Machine code	The language of binary numbers in which a processor works (or, to some, the equivalent code in hexadecimal form or even assembler).
Machine intelligence	Some programs are intelligent in that if humans were to do the same work, you would call them intelligent. See also expert systems.
Machine readable	Data in a form of a suitable input device that can transfer a copy into a computer.
Magnetic ink character reader (MICR)	A device for reading (machine readable) magnetic ink characters into main store.
Magnetic media	Media on which a system can store data in the form of a magnetic record; tapes, disks and stripe cards in particular.
Main store	Where a system keeps instructions and data ready for immediate access.
Mainframe	A large powerful computer able to handle the needs of many, often remote, users and to work with various programs in the same time.
Maintenance	File maintenance.
Mark sensor/reader	An input device able to convert information held as marks on the source document to data.
Master file	A file in a data bank currently available for access, rather than a backup copy or one for holding new transactions.
Medium	The actual substance or item which stores data.

Memory	Data store.
Merge	Combine two files (eg master file and transaction file) into one for future use.
Mesh network	Network design in which the stations link direct to each other.
MICR	Magnetic ink character reader.
Micro(computer)	A fairly small computer used by only one person at a time.
Microform	Microfilm or fiche, able to store pages of data as tiny images.
Microprocessor	A processor on a single chip.
Mini(computer)	Cheaper and more compact than a mainframe and more likely than a micro to have several users at once.
Modem	A device that allows digital units like fax machines and computers to transfer data into and from an analogue system, in particular the telephone network.
Monitor	A high quality visual output unit with a steady clear display.
Mouse	Input device which you roll round on a surface to control the movement of a pointer on screen; pressing buttons on the mouse causes action.
Multi-access	Multi-user.
Multiplexing	Treating two or more signals so they can pass through a channel at the same time.
Multiprocessing	A system with two or more processors working in parallel, sharing tasks and providing support for each other.
Multiprogramming	A system which runs more than one program during a given period by timesharing, switching between them from moment to moment.
Multitasking	Describes a concurrent system — one that can handle two or more programs at a time.
Multiuser	A system that can handle the needs of more than one user at a time.

Network	System for linking IT units so they can communicate with each other and (in the case of computers) share facil*ies like disk drives and printers.
Object program	A machine code program produced by an assembler or compiler and ready to run.
OCR	Optical character reader.
Off-line	Describes a hardware device not at the moment linked to and controlled by a computer, but resting or carrying out its own processing locally.
Office	Centre for handling information to meet human needs. Office automation involves using IT to improve efficiency.
OMR	Optical mark reader.
On-line	Connected to and under the control of a working computer system, locally or remotely through a telecommunications link.
Operating software (OS)	The program(s) in overall control of a computer system, without which the system would be useless.
Operations manager	The person in charge of the day-to-day running of a large computer.
Operator	A person with the task of keeping a large computer system working.
Optical	To do with light, whose waves have very high frequencies compared with radio, and so give far greater information carrying capacity. Compact and video disks are optical too — they store data so a beam of laser light can read it.
Optical character reader (OCR)	An input device able to recognise the shapes of characters, which are in human readable form.
Optical mark reader (OMR)	An input device for reading marks in given places on special forms.
Output	Any result produced by an IT system — usually text andlor graphics shown on screen and printed on paper for human use, or signals to one or more control units in the case of an automated system.

Package	Program or suite complete with documentation (and perhaps hardware) designed for a particular application.
Packet	A chunk of data prepared for rapid transfer through a local or public network.
Paddle	Joystick.
Page printer	A fast quiet printer that in effect constructs for output a page at a time.
Parallel processing	When two or more processors of roughly equal status share a task by working on parts at the same time, the same as multiprocessing.
Parallel transfer	When the bits of a byte pass along a bundle of lines together rather than serially.
Pascal	A general purpose high-level program language that offers good data structure features, widely used with learners.
PBX	Private branch exchange.
PC	Personal computer, especially one that works in much the same way as the IBM type.
Peripheral	Any computer hardware item other than the processor — input/loutput device or backing storage unit in particular.
Personal computer	A computer small or cheap enough for use mainly by one person.
PL11	Program language number 1, a high-level program language of value in both business and scientific contexts.
Plotter	An output device for drawing graphics and lettering in which a computer directly controls the movement of one or more pens over the paper (see drum and flat bed).
Point of sale (POS)	The place where a shop transaction occurs (eg a checkout).
Printout	Hard copy output from a computer printer.
Private branch exchange (PBX)	A local telephone exchange (switching centre), installed on your own premises and run by your own staff.

Processor	The part of a computer that actually does the arithmetic and makes the decisions, sometimes called central processing unit (CPU) and a micro (often called a microprocessor).
Program	An ordered list of instructions for a system to follow and carry out a given task. (See also stored program).
Program language	System for giving special instructions to computers (which have to translate programs written, turning them into machine code before they can follow the instructions). A program generator is a program that can take your ideas and produce a working program.
Programmer	A person whose task is to produce instructions that a computer can follow from an algorithm devised during systems analysis.
PROM	Programmable read only memory (store), is a chip programmed by a user rather than by the maker.
RAM	A form of storage used in computers (random access memory).
Random access	Direct access.
Read and write	Describes any data you can both read from and write to, such as a note book, random access memory and an unprotected disk.
Read and write memory	Storage space inside a computer for holding data while in use, whose contents are constantly overwritten as different programs run. This is temporary storage and will disappear when you switch off.
Read only	Describes data you can read from, but not write, such as a text book, ROM, and a protected disk.
Read only memory (ROM)	The part of a system's main store for software in frequent use — it is not volatile and you cannot write to it.
Real-time	A system that reacts to each input it receives quickly enough to be able to affect the source of the input, eg in control or (almost real-time) interactive work.
Real time clock	Keeps a count of day, date and time for use with filing and/or display.

Record	A file, the data on one entity (eg car part, client).
Register	A small special-purpose store (with no more than a few cells) in a processor, for holding data during processing.
Remote job entry	Using a remote console or terminal to send job instructions to a multiprocessing computer.
Report	(a) A user defined summary of, or extract from, information held in a database, and a report generator being a program to extract, sort and collate information. (b) Computer output telling the user of problems met during a job.
Resolution	Measures the quality of printout and computer displays and graphics. For instance, the higher the resolution the finer the detail.
Ring	A network laid out in a loop.
ROM	Read only memory.
Scheduler	The part of operating software which looks after sharing out time between tasks in timesharing contexts.
Screen	Output device such as a monitor or flat liquid crystal display.
Sector	A physical unit (block or physical record) of disk storage, its size being a factor of the track length.
Security	Keeping data safe from loss and corruption.
Semi-compilation	The translation of a program in a language such as Forth, with a small interpreter as well as a compiler.
Semiconductor chip	Scrap of semiconductor (eg silicon) with microelectronic circuits built into the surface, used as a data store.
Sensor	Device that detects touch, temperature, sound, acidity or other similar (analogue) physical or chemical information, with a corresponding electrical output able to allow comupters and robots to react to their environment.
Sequential	A sequential file having the records in key field value order.

Serial	(a) For data transfer where the bits of a byte pass along a single line one after the other (compare parallel)
	(b) As a physical file where the records come one after the other, but in no special order (compare sequential)
Software	The programs and data used to drive a system (operating software) to carry out a task (application or language software).
Sort	To put the records of a data file in the order of current needs .
Source document	A piece of paper that contains information ready for input to a computer.
Source program	The set of instructions produced (in assembly or high-level language) before translation (assembly or compilation) to the machine code object program for execution by an interpreter.
Speech recognition	Using software to allow computer input of spoken data and commands.
Speech synthesis	The production by software through a speaker of sounds like human speech.
Spreadsheet	A business software package that displays a grid of entries (such as accounts) and allows you to work on the relationships between them, showing at once the effects of changes.
Star	Also called cluster, a simple layout (eg network) whose links radiate from the centre.
Store	To hold data for later use, or the place where it is held. An IT system having three main levels of storage (internal registers, immediate access main store and backing store).
Stored program concept	A major aspect of the modern computer — it can store in main memory the set of instructions it needs to carry out, so the system can branch andlor modify the instructions during a run.
Structure	The layout of system or program, a structure chart showing how the parts relate.
Synchronous	A signal whose packets transfer in response to commands from outside.

System	A set of hardware/software/people, or a set of working procedures to carry out a given task.
Systems analysis	Analysing an information handling need and working out what systems would best meet it.
Systems software	Software like the operating software and program languages a system needs for it to do anything useful.
Tape	Magnetically or optically coated plastic tape used for holding data for access by a suitable drive.
Telecommunications	Transfer of information or data over a distance.
Terminal	Hardware combining input and output units to let the user communicate with a remote system.
Testing	Checking a program or system for faults, using carefully thought-out methods and data.
Timesharing	Letting a processor work on several jobs at once, by sharing its time in turn between them (perhaps with fixed length slices) as in multiprogramming and multiuser systems.
Trace	(a) To dry run an algorithm giving most attention to data item values (putting them in a trace table).
	(b) To have a system output the details of its route through a program.
Track	A linear (on a tape) or circular (on a disk) space for laying down data.
Tracker ball	The same effect as a mouse or joystick.
Transaction file	A file of a firm's transactions, with each transaction record being added after the last, in random order.
Transistor	Small semiconductor device used for switching and amplifying signals.
Unix	A multiuser, multitasking operating software system, effective both with a very large storage demand, and with shells needed for an accessible user interface.
User friendly	Describes IT systems easy to learn and to use by people like those for whom they are designed.

User interface	The mode of interaction between a system and a user, and its associated hardware and software.
Utilities	Programs that let you do useful jobs like backing up disks and editing the contents of main store.
Valve	Out-dated electronic signal switching and amplifying device based on current in a vacuum.
VDU	(See Visual Display Unit.)
Virtual storage	A method of getting main store to hold larger programs or more data than normal, by loading certain blocks from backing store.
Visual display unit (VDU)	A device that displays computer output on a screen, also used loosely to mean a combined screen and keyboard unit (workstation or terminal).
Voice recognition unit	A computer input device you can train to identify spoken words (see also speech).
Wide area network	Network that links computers and terminals spread over a large distance (eg a whole country).
Word	A system's basic unit of data processing — a byte in the case of an 8-bit machine, a double byte with a 16-bit machine, etc.
Word processing	A system for entering, editing, laying out, printing and storing text comparable to desk top publishing
Workstation	Where a user interacts with a network.

Appendix 2
Bibliography

Barden, R A; *How to Start in Office Automation* (NCC Blackwell, 1988).

Blacklock, P; *Computer Programming* 2nd edition (NCC Blackwell, 1993).

Collin, W G; *Introducing Computer Programming* (NCC Publications, 1978).

Date, C J; *An Introduction to Database Systems* (Addison Wesley, 1986).

Devargas, M; *Local Area Networks* (NCC Blackwell, 1992)

Gandy, M; *Choosing a Local Area Network* (NCC Blackwell, 1985).

Marlow, A.J; *What is Desktop Publishing?* (NCC Blackwell, 1990)

Skidmore, *Introducing Systems Analysis*, 2nd edition, (NCC Blackwell, 1994)

Appendix 3
Examination Questions

The questions below are taken from past NCC Diploma examinations.

QUESTION 1—JUNE 1989

Briefly explain the following:

a) RJE

b) CAI or CAL or CBL

c) QBE

d) MIS

Describe one major difference between the following:

e) MICROFILM and MICROFICHE

f) MODULATE and DEMODULATE

g) DUPLEX and HALF-DUPLEX Transmission

h) EVEN PARITY and ODD PARITY

i) PARALLEL and SERIAL Transmission

j) WORK FILE and MASTER FILE

Give two reasons why:

k) PASSWORDS are required

l) STANDARDS are set

m) AUDIT TRAILS are kept

n) SPOOLERS are used

QUESTION 2—JUNE 1989

a) The use of computers in industry and commerce has greatly changed the ways in which people work. This is particularly noticeable to the general public in large supermarkets.

List three types of COMPUTER APPLICATION which you might find in use in a large supermarket, explain the tasks they perform and how they are INTEGRATED into the whole system.

b)   Write short notes on three of the following:

   i)   EFTPOS

   ii)   EFTS

   iii) PIN

   iv)   CAD/CAM

QUESTION 3—SEPTEMBER 1989

Briefly explain the following computing terms:

a)   INTERRUPT

b)   EXPERT SYSTEMS

c)   RELATIONAL DATABASE

d)   FIRMWARE

e)   FRONT END PROCESSOR

f)   OBJECT CODE

g)   SYSTEMS SOFTWARE

Explain the differences between the following:

h)   PARALLEL and SERIAL TRANSMISSION

i)   RANDOM files and INDEX-SEQUENTIAL files

j)   SEEK TIME and ROTATIONAL DELAY (latency)

k)   PACKET switching and CIRCUIT switching

l)   THIRD and FOURTH GENERATION languages

m)   COMPILERS and INTERPRETERS

n)   EPROM and PROM

QUESTION 4 — SEPTEMBER 1989

Within the computer ALL INFORMATION is represented by various BINARY CODES. With the help of simple examples explain how the computer represents:

a)   CHARACTERS

b)   FIXED POINT numbers

c)   FLOATING POINT numbers

d)   INSTRUCTIONS

QUESTION 5 — SEPTEMBER 1989

It is essential that data entering the computer system should be correct:

a)   Explain the operation of a KEY-TO-DISK system and indicate its advantages over a commonly used earlier system of the data entry

b)   With the help of examples describe how PARITY BITS and CHECK DIGITS are used to monitor the correctness of data.

QUESTION 6 — SEPTEMBER 1989

A branch of a large engineering company specialises in the design of printed circuit boards. At present the designs are hand drawn and then sent by post to the main office. Company policy is now to computerise these activities in both the main and the branch offices.

a)   Suggest a suitable HARDWARE CONFIGURATION for the new computer system giving reasons for your choice.

b)   What advantages is the computerised system likely to have over the present manual system?

QUESTION 7 — JANUARY 1990

Define the following abbreviations and explain, in one sentence, how, why or when they are used or applied:

a)   FEP

b)   DOS

c)   MIS

d)   ISAM

e)   ATM

f)   PROLOG

g)   VLSI

What is the difference between each of the following pairs of items?

h)   TRANSPOSITION ERRORS and TRANSCRIPTION ERRORS

i)   TRUNCATION and ROUNDING

j)   BYTE and WORD

k)   COMPILER and ASSEMBLER

1)   CAD and CAM

m)   ASCII and EBCDIC

n)   INTEGER and REAL

QUESTION 8—JANUARY 1990

A DATABASE is an essential part of a large organisation.

a)   The ORGANISATION of DATA in a database has THREE major objectives. State and describe each.

b)   List SIX features of a DBMS (Database Management System) and briefly describe each.

QUESTION 9—JANUARY 1990

When data is entered into a computer system it must be correct.

a)   Identify SIX data VALIDATION checks and show how each can be applied to a DATE field in the form (dd/mm/yyyy).

b) Explain the operation of a KEY-TO-DISK system and how it may help to improve data quality.

QUESTION 10—JANUARY 1990

In the development of a RELIABLE computer system adherence to STANDARDS plays a significant role.

a)   What objectives do we try to achieve by the use of standards?

b)   What standards can be applied to:

   i)   PROGRAM DOCUMENTATION?

   ii) The production of SOURCE CODE?

Index